Scotch & Water

NEIL WILSON PUBLISHING • GLASGOW • SCOTLAND

Neil Wilson Publishing Ltd
303a The Pentagon Centre
36 Washington Street
GLASGOW G3 8AZ
Tel: 0141-221-1117 Fax: 0141-221-5363
E-mail: nwp@cqm.co.uk http://www.nwp.co.uk/
© Neil Wilson, 1985, 1989, 1992, 1998
Foreword © Charles MacLean, 1998

The author has established his moral right to be identified as the author of this work. A catalogue record for this book is available from the British Library.
First published by Lochar Publishing, Lockerbie, 1985
Second edition published by Lochar Publishing, Moffat, 1989
Second edition re-issued by Neil Wilson Publishing, Glasgow, 1992
Third edition published by Neil Wilson Publishing, Glasgow, 1998
ISBN 1-897784-58-9   Printed in China

Dedicated to the memory of Freda Ramsay of Kildalton

The original edition of 1985 received assistance from Isle of Jura and Bowmore distilleries towards the cost of promotion.

CONTENTS

ACKNOWLEDGEMENTS

The author and the publisher would like to thank the following people for their enthusiasm and encouragement in the preparation of *Scotch and Water*: Freda Ramsay of Kildalton; David Daiches; Donald Mackinlay, Sally Galloway and Pam Brough of Charles Mackinlay & Co Ltd; Tim Morrison, Joe Hughes, Mr H Cockburn and George Hocknull of Stanley P Morrison Ltd; John Burns of Invergordon Distillers; Iain Wilson of Long John International Ltd; Gordon McIntosh of White Horse Distillers Ltd; the late Allan McArthur and Allan Meikle of Highland Distilleries;Mr A H Barclay of Hiram Walker & Sons; Stewart Jowett and Bob Buglass of Tobermory Distillers; Mr T J Brooke, Alan Tait, Jeff Lodge, Michael Braithwaite and Miss Leslie Holloway of the Distillers Company plc; John Bulman of Jura Distillery; Jim McEwan of Bowmore; Murdo Reed of Laphroaig; Don Raitt of Ardbeg; Alastair Robertson of Lagavulin; Ernie Cattanach of Port Ellen Maltings; Ian Allan of Bruichladdich; Grant Carmichael of Caol Ila; Douglas Bottomer of Talisker; W Delmé-Evans; Tommy Williamson; Richard Grindal of the Scotch Whisky Association; Graham Taylor of Glen Catrine Bonded Warehouse Ltd; Hugh Currie of St Andrews Distilling Co; Duncan Macrae of the Caledonian Distillery; Sheila Burtles and Robert Pass of the Pentlands Scotch Whisky Research Association; Brian Smith of the East of Scotland Agricultural College; Ian Lochrie and John Fox of the Glenlight Shipping Co; Davy Langlands and the crew of the *Pibroch*; Norman McCandlish at BBC Scotland; Allan Craig; Merlin Currie, John Hooker and Ian Anderson; Eddie Holmes of the Scottish Tourist Board; Charlie Maclean of MacleanDubois; Robin Hodge; Max Macleod; Iain Thornber of Lochailort; Malcolm Tarrell; John Musto; Callum Neish and Chris Hindmarsh; Mr and Mrs Taylor and family of the Dower House Hotel, Islay; Neil Carmichael of Bowmore; Sandy MacCormick; David Bell; the patrons of the White Hart Hotel, Port Ellen; Hugh MacInness; Alan Hyslop, Micky Heads, Alec Johnston and Peter McGregor of Laphroaig; Mrs Macmillan of Tallant; Gordon Booth and the curators of the Islay Museum of Life; Robbie Currie; Lord Margadale; the staff and patrons of the Port Askaig Hotel; Gordon Wright of the Jura Hotel; Mr F A Riley-Smith; Jock Paton; Mrs Margaret Nelson of Ardlussa and her son Jamie; Neil MacInness; Viscount Astor; Bill Dunn; Tony Tucker; Murdo MacDonald the archivist for Argyll and Bute District Council; Mr and Mrs Bell, Tobermory; John MacLeod of MacLeod; Mrs Gouldesborough, Mr Hill and the staff of the Scottish Records Office; the staff of the Scottish Reference Room, Central Library, Edinburgh; Ian Wilson and his wife Jacky; Keith Johnstone and Roger Houston of Criffel Micro Business Systems, Dumfries; Douglas MacVean and his staff at Moffat Woollens Ltd; Michael Moss of the Glasgow University Archives; Geoffrey Quick and Mr Hay of the Royal Commission on the Ancient and Historical Monuments of Scotland; Kate McQueen; Mrs Margaret McEwan; Annie Dana of the Scotch Malt Whisky Society; D K Shiels & Staff of the Tartan Gift Shops Ltd, Edinburgh and Moffat; Ladbrokes Hotels Ltd; Col 'Timber' Wood of the Argyll and Sutherland Highlanders; The Malt Distillers Association of Scotland; Dr John Lorne Campbell of Canna; Helen Watson of the Scottish National Portrait Gallery; Kate Middleton of the George Washington Wilson Collection, Aberdeen University; the crew of the *Alystra*, ably skippered by Tony Gill aided by his wife Anya – Neil Wilson, Mike De Luca, Allan Wright, Lincoln Rowe and Steve Johnston; a special thanks to the people of Islay, Jura, Mull and Skye without whom it would not have been worthwhile.

Picture Credits

Steve Johnston 2-3, 17, 20, 27, 28, 31,36, 40, 43, 48, 50, 78, 80, 82, 104, 110; National Galleries of Scotland, Edinburgh 10, 123; Freda Ramsay 15 (Painting by Sir Daniel MacNee), 46, 65; Allan Wright Front cover, 17, 19, 26, 32, 33, 36, 38-39, 46, 52, 61, 70, 73, 74, 75, 79, 86, 87, 88-89, 90-91, 98-99, 102, 103, 111; Photograph by Eric Thorburn 20 (Islay House), 22; Nigel Jones Illustration on p24-25; Allan Marshall 25; Ardbeg Distillery 6, 30, 43, 70; Neil Wilson 17, 28, 31, 33, 45, 48, 74, 110, 116, 117, 118, 121, 122-123, 124; Hiram Walker & Sons (Scotland) plc 43; Long John International Ltd 53, 54, 55, 56, 57, 58, 59, 60; Geraldine Edgar Illustration on p 54; Tommy Williamson 67; The British Library 68 (Etching by J Cleaveley Jun, 1772) 91 (Etching by John Frederick Miller, 1772), Islay Museums Trust 70; Stanley P Morrison Ltd 76-77, 90; The Distillers Company plc 80, 90, 120; Invergordon Distillers Ltd 86; Reproduced by kind permission of The Highland Distilleries plc 89; Isle of Jura Distillery Ltd 96; Charles Mackinlay & Co Ltd 101; Aberdeen University Library, G W Wilson Collection 6, 108, 113, 120.

Author's Note to 1998 edition.
I have left the acknowledgements exactly as they were published in the revised 1989 edition (which was re-issued in 1992) because they detail the many contacts who were kind enough to help me when originally researching this book. Sadly many of them have passed on, including Freda Ramsay of Kildalton whose knowledge on distilling matters on Islay was unequalled.

FOREWORD

SCOTCH AND WATER IS A CLASSIC. IT IS ONE OF ONLY A handful of books about Scotch whisky published in the last twenty years which breaks new ground, based upon detailed original research, and offers new insight into its subject, rather than just rehashing old material.

It was first published in 1985, ten years after my father sold his yacht. For I, like Neil, used to ply the waters of the Hebrides in my youth, in search of adventure, wilderness and drams. On one occasion, after a hard day's sailing, we moored in Port Ellen harbour and ended up drinking a little too much Islay whisky. Over the next year I struggled to keep down any whisky having a peat reek! On another occasion, we were bribed with a bottle of Grouse to leave the douce guests of the Motor Inn at Loch Melfort in peace. If only *Scotch and Water* had been available to us then: it would not only have enriched our experience but also given purpose to our island sea-roving.

For this book is about more than just whisky. It is about the communities in the islands that made and still make the stuff. Whisky — and everything to do with it — runs like a golden thread through the fabric of these places, both today and in the past. Indeed, one might go so far as to say that this thread links the communities to their history. As Professor David Daiches wrote in his foreword to the first edition of this book:

The history [of malt whisky] *is bound up in all sorts of ways with the rhythms of life and work in Scottish communities. To know about Scotch whisky is not only to have acquired a certain connoisseurship; it is also to know about some important aspects of Scotland's past and present.*

Neil Wilson's feeling for Scotland and the Scots people — past and present — is as strong as his feeling for Scotch whisky. His knowledge, understanding and sympathy for all three is profound, and informs every page of *Scotch and Water*. I am delighted he is reissuing it, and commend it to you warmly.

Charles MacLean, Edinburgh, January 1998

GLOSSARY

Alcohol

Alcohol accumulates whenever yeast ferments and since yeast cannot utilise alcohol, it becomes one of the major by-products of fermentation which may be summarised as:

$$C_6H_{12}O_6 \rightarrow 2C_2H_5OH + 2CO_2$$

Glucose   Ethanol   Carbon Dioxide

Aquavitae

The Latin for 'water of life' from which the Gaelic 'uisge beatha' and 'usquebaugh' were derived. The modern 'whisky' is a simple corruption of 'usque'.

Barm

Yeast.

Bear, bere, bigg

The strain of four-rowed barley in common use throughout the islands and Western Highlands until superseded, as the Rev James MacDonald observed in 1810 '. . . with the real barley with long two row grained ears. The reason urged for preferring the inferior species to the better kind is, that it is fourteen days or three weeks earlier in ripening, and that it does not require such rich manure, or as fertile a soil as the genuine barley.'

Bere

See Bear

Boll

Chambers 20th Century Dictionary defines a boll as equal to six Imperial bushels. In reality it was an arbitrary unit used to measure grain, but generally the measures in common use were

1 boll = 6 bushels
1 bushel = 8 gallons
1 peck = 2 gallons.

Duntuilm Castle.

Bond

Whisky stocks held in bonded warehouses have yet to have Excise duty levied upon them.

Bourbon

Bourbon whiskey is produced from a mash of not less than 51% corn grain. Bourbon casks are charcoaled to impart flavour to the maturing spirit.

Burnt ale, pot ale

The liquor left in the low wines or wash still after the first distillation. It is either discharged as waste, or converted into animal feed.

Bushel

Traditionally the dry measure of 8 Imperial gallons, although the SWA regard it as equivalent to 25.4 kg.

Butt

See casks.

Casks

Constructed of oak, casks used for whisky maturation come in various sizes:

Butt . . . 500 litres
Hogshead . . . 250–305 litres
American Barrel . . . 173–191 litres
Quarter . . . 127–159 litres
Octave . . . 45–68 litres

Cistern

The latter-day equivalent of the steep.

Couch frame

The apparatus in which barley was stored prior to

Filling casks at Ardbeg c. 1912.

steeping.

Draff

The spent grist left in the mashtun after mashing is completed. Excellent cattle food.

Dram

In Gaelic – a drink.

Drawback

A rebate or reduction in the level of duty commonly applied to malt made from bear in the 19th Century.

Dun

In Gaelic, a fort or castle.

Dunnage

The traditional means of racking casks in warehouses. Two wooden rails are laid along the top of a row of casks and the next row rolled into position along the rails. Each cask is secured in place with wooden wedges on either side. Although it appears precarious, dunnage is still in common use in many warehouses in Scotland.

Enzymes

Complex chemical compounds which help to break down the starch within the endosperm into sugars during germination.

Ethanol

The primary alcohol produced during the fermentation of yeast.

Feu

Land held in perpetuity in payment of a yearly rental.

Genever, Holland's gin

The Dutch national drink which takes it name from the French for juniper — genièvre. Not dissimilar to gin.

Grain whisky

Whisky which is produced by the patent still continuous process. It differs in a number of ways from malt whisky. The mash consists of a proportion of malted barley along with unmalted cereals. The unmalted cereals are cooked under steam pressure for some 3½ hours (which causes the starch cells to burst) before they are transferred to the mashtun. The enzymes from the malted barley portion then convert the starch into sugar.

The wort produced in this manner is of a lower specific gravity than in the case of the malt whisky process and the spirit collected from the patent still is of a much higher strength.

Haircloth

Spread over the kiln floor to prevent the barley dropping onto the peat furnace below. In modern distilleries a metal grating serves the same purpose.

Hogshead

See casks.

Lyne arm

The part of the pot still extending from the top of the neck down to the condenser.

Octave

See casks.

Piece

The name given to the germinating barley on the floor of the malting house.

Pot ale

See burnt ale.

Lyne arms entering worm tubs.

Proof

Proof spirit at 51°F weighs exactly twelve-thirteenths of a volume of distilled water equal to the volume of spirit. Effectively, proof spirit contains 57.1% spirit and 42.9% water. The strength of whisky is now measured as the percentage of alcohol by volume at 20°C. In the United States a proof system is still operated whereby 100° American Proof equates to 50% alcoholic volume.

Quarter

See casks.

Sparge

The name given to the liquor from the final water of the mash. It is used as the first water of the next mash.

Specific gravity

The density of a given substance, in the case of spirits it is measured in grams per cubic centimetre.

Surfactant

A substance which reduces surface tension and thus foaming and frothing.

Switchers

Rotating arms employed to reduce frothing in washbacks during fermentation.

Triple distillation

Simply another stage of distillation added to the normal double distillation common throughout Scotland. Only Springbank, Auchentoshan and Rosebank still employ the technique and Talisker stopped it in 1928. All Irish distilleries use triple distillation.

Uisge beatha, usquebaugh

In Gaelic – water of life. See aquavitae.

Vatted malt

A mixture of single malt whiskies either from different distilleries or from the same distillery but of differing ages.

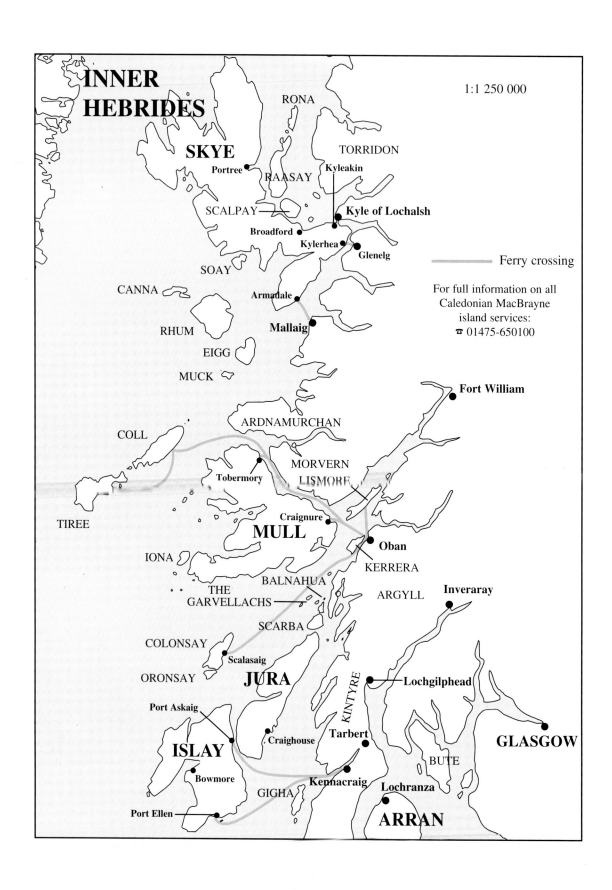

CHAPTER ONE

A BARBAROUS PEOPLE

THIS ISLAND HATH A LIBERTY of brewing whisky . . .', wrote the Reverend Archibald Robertson in 1793 in his Parish report for Kildalton, Islay in the Old Statistical Account of Scotland. His observation was no exaggeration, and arouses as much curiosity in the amateur historian as it does in any visitor to the island. On studying a modern day map of the Inner Hebrides the question arises, 'Why so many distilleries on Islay?', for there are eight in all, and to the north another on Jura, one on Mull, and another on Skye.

At first glance, these 11 distilleries appear to be unusual places in which to establish and conduct business, being found in remote and unlikely settings, far removed from the mainland centres of commerce. The reasons for their existence are many but not too obscure. They may be traced with the unwitting help of some of the great scholars, academics and travellers of the past few centuries who made the Hebrides a subject of their letters and books, leaving us many insights into the lives and customs of the islanders.

Their names are part of established Hebridean literature – Martin Martin, Thomas Pennant, Sam Johnson, John Knox, the Reverend James Macdonald,

Alfred Barnard, John MacCulloch, Hugh Miller, Joseph Mitchell, John Ramsay and the many Ministers of the Church of Scotland whose Parish reports formed those most remarkable commentaries on society, the Old and New Statistical Accounts of 1794 and 1844.

Islay, as the most southerly of the Hebridean islands, lies within 17 miles (27.2 km) of the coast of Ireland, and as early as the 6th Century the Scots had crossed into Argyll from Ireland and established the new territory of Dalriada. In AD 678, they clashed in battle with the Britons on Jura and in AD 719, two Dalriad tribes opposed each other on Gigha. Having firmly established themselves and uniting with the Picts around AD 843, the Scots gradually gave their name to the new nation which largely adopted their Celtic form of speech.

Some 600 years later the art of distillation is believed to have been carried over the same water to Islay, an island eminently well suited to its execution with unlimited supplies of peat, burns running brim-full with soft water and a fertile soil for that most vital ingredient – grain. The intervening years had brought the Hebrides under the rule of the Norwegian

Crown which, after the unsuccessful expedition of King Haco in 1263 to maintain sovereignty, finally ceded the islands 3 years later to King Alexander III of Scotland. By that time, however, they were Norwegian in name alone, for their control had been effectively destroyed in the 12th Century by Somerled, from whom the Lords of the Isles were descended. One of Somerled's grandsons, Donald, started the great house of Macdonald which assumed the Lordship until 1493 when, through their recklessness and rebellion, they forfeited both the title and their lands to the Scottish Crown.

The Macdonalds' dominion had never been firmly established, for the islands were habitually in the hands of several clans, all of them powerful and some of them none too well disposed to each other. The MacLeans of Duart on Mull were in possession of lands granted them by John Macdonald, Lord of the Isles, in 1366 through the marriage of his daughter to Lachlan Lubanach MacLean of Duart. Other MacLean factions held between them much of Mull, Tiree, Jura, Scarba, Lochaber, Coll and Rhum. The two families of MacLeod held Lewis and Harris whilst sharing Skye and Raasay. Similarly, the MacNeils were two independent families living on Barra and Gigha, while the Macdonalds held Islay, the seat of the Lord of the Isles.

Over the course of the 16th Century these clans literally lived in their own world, oblivious to the sovereignty of the Scottish Crown, warring amongst themselves, exacting their own form of justice and frequently settling arguments with the sword. Raiding was common and profitable; MacLean of Duart plundered Gigha in 1579 returning to Mull with no less than 500 head of cattle and 2,000 sheep and goats. A long-standing feud with the Macdonalds was finally settled in 1598 at Gruinart, Islay, the MacLeans returning to Duart with their tails firmly between their legs.

Distilling was by then an established practice in the islands, the product being a coarse brew, drawn from local cereals such

*T*he Marquess of Huntly (above) would have become one of Scotland's most famous mass-murderers had he not incurred the wrath of the Presbytereans on King James' Privy Council in the early 17th Century.

as oats. A hefty draught of this 'aquavitae' would have given an eager warrior greater heart in those troubled times and probably hospitalised an ordinary mortal today. When the fighting eventually subsided King James VI demanded that MacLean and Macdonald come to Edinburgh to discuss the future of the Isles. Unwittingly, they walked into a trap and were imprisoned in Edinburgh Castle where they naturally begged for mercy. Surprisingly, King James let them off on condition that they behave themselves. A few years later they returned to the King's favour when they agreed to contribute more to the Treasury by increasing the amount due for the rent of their lands, which Macdonald, of course, had had to pay since the forfeiture of 1493.

Not for the first time King James' warning went unheeded as the Isles remained lawless, harbouring criminals and smugglers alike. The Stewart succession to the English throne complicated James' efforts to find a solution when the Royal Court was removed to London in March 1603. He believed adamantly in the Union of Crowns and of a united Britain, desiring 'a perfect Union of Laws and Persons, and such a Naturalising as may make one body of both Kingdoms under me your King . . .'. In relentless pursuit of this ideal he decided to finally rid himself of the rebellious inhabitants of the Isles and in 1607, totally exasperated, he agreed to nothing less than the extermination of the entire island population. This unbelievable proposal, of which many Scots remain ignorant, was to be carried out by the Marquess of Huntly, who was given one year in which to 'extirpate the barbarous people of the Isles . . .'.

The Marquess however, was a Catholic, and being a powerful man he naturally attracted the attention of the Presbyterians who managed to have him confined by the Privy Council to the burgh of Elgin and its environs. Fortunately for the islanders, whilst so restrained he was unable to carry out his bloody mission, and unfortunately for the Marquess he was constantly exposed to the sermons of zealous Presbyterian preachers in the hope that he might renounce the Church of Rome.

In 1608 King James again tried to force any rebellious chiefs into submission by sending an overpowering fleet under the charge of his Lieutenant, Lord Ochiltree, to intimidate the island strongholds into submission. The fleet took the Macdonald's Dunyveg Castle by Lagavulin followed by the inland fortress on Loch Gorm before moving quickly north to Mull, where MacLean of Duart, realising the extent of the fleet, as it anchored in the Bay of Torosay, surrendered.

Ochiltree then moved up the Sound of Mull to Aros, near Salen, to hold court with the island chiefs. They included Donald MacAllan, Captain of Clanranald, Donald Gorm MacDonald of Sleat, Ruairidh MacLeod of Harris, Hector and Lachlan MacLean of Duart and Angus Macdonald of Dunyveg, who immediately pledged himself once more to the Crown and returned to Islay forthwith. Ochiltree remained suspicious of the others and took counsel from the Bishop of the Isles who was present; together they masterminded a piece of pure theatre for the unsuspecting chiefs. All but MacLeod of Harris, who may have smelt a rat and managed to return home, were invited to hear a sermon from the Bishop and then retire to dine aboard Ochiltree's ship, *The Moon*. When assembled there, and doubtless plied with a few drinks, Ochiltree announced, 'Gentlemen, I have the honour, as his Majesty's Lieutenant of the Isles, to inform you that you are now his Majesty's prisoners.' And with that, the ship weighed anchor and sailed for Ayr, where the Privy Council despatched the chiefs to a number of scattered castle dungeons until their lesson had been learnt.

If King James thought that he was finally making some headway against the island chiefs, he made sure the point was not lost and pressed home his advantage. In 1609 he appointed the Bishop of the Isles to enact a number of Statutes at Iona (or Icolmkill), outlining proposals deemed necessary by his commission to create a civilised society throughout the Isles. This comprehensive survey of social design reflected the state of life in the Isles in the late 16th and early 17th Centuries and gave valuable insights into what King James and the Privy Council considered to be root evils prevalent at the time – needless to say, drink was one of them. Once more the chiefs were assembled to hear the Bishop who this time preached far more than a mere sermon.

Bishop Andrew began with a subject dear to his heart, namely the Kirk. The First Statute proposed that those Ministers set down in each island parish 'shall be reverently obeyed, their stipends dutifully paid them, the ruinous kirks with reasonable diligence repaired, the sabbath solemnly kept, and committers of adultery, fornication and incest severely punished.' Handfasting, that is the testing of fertility before a marriage was solemnised, was also declared illegal. Martin Martin explained this in 1703: *I*T WAS AN ANCIENT CUSTOM IN *the Isles that a man take a maid to his wife, and keep her for the space of a year without marrying her; and if she pleased him all the while, he married her at the end of the year, and* *legitimized her children; but if he did not love her, he returned her to her parents.*

Perfectly straightforward one would think, but King James was no fool for outlawing handfasting since he was well aware of what happened in Skye in 1599. That year Donald Gorm handfasted with Margaret MacLeod, the sister of Ruairidh, and bore her away to Duntuilm Castle. Things did not go too well between them and when Margaret injured her eye, Donald Gorm decided he had had enough and sent her back to Dunvegan. He did this in an extremely unsubtle manner, for Margaret arrived home riding a one-eyed horse, attended by a one-eyed groom and followed by a one-eyed mangy dog. Ruairidh was incensed and all hell broke loose. The ensuing 'War of the One-Eyed Woman' lasted 2 years, ending in the rout of the MacLeods at Coire na Creiche above Glen Brittle. Thankfully, it did at least signal the end of clan fights in Skye.

The Second Statute had a more profound effect on the landscape for it proposed the establishment of inns and hostelries in convenient places within every isle, selling food and drink at reasonable prices. Many change-houses were thereafter built at junctions and ferry points along the length of the drove roads which carried the island cattle to the mainland markets.

The Third Statute forbade the presence of malingerers who had no means or occupation within the Isles, and limited the number of gentlemen whom each chief could entertain in his household. Macdonald of Dunyveg, Donald Gorm MacDonald, Ruairidh MacLeod, and Donald MacAllan were limited to six, MacLean of Duart eight, and the lesser men three.

Under the Fourth Statute beggars and sorners who, until then had existed by the ancient right of extracting maintenance from the common folk, were banished unless they could pay for their needs at one of the inns.

The chiefs were probably not too worried at this point, but the worst was yet to come. Bishop Andrew claimed under the Fifth Statute that 'one of the special causes of the great poverty of the said Isles, and of the great cruelty and inhuman barbarity practised by sundry of the inhabitants of the same upon others their natural friends and neighbours, has been the extraordinary drinking of strong wines and aquavitae brought in amongst them, partly by merchants of the mainland and partly by some traffickers dwelling amongst themselves.' This, the Bishop deemed would have to stop, and he proposed that importation of spirits cease, and that anyone found smuggling should pay 40 Scots pounds for the first offence, rising to 100 pounds for the second, with a third and final offence resulting in the forfeiture of all buildings, goods and possessions. But most surprisingly of all, and this demonstrates how great a factor drink was in Hebridean society, the Statute demurred '. . . without prejudice always to any person within the said Isles to brew aquavitae and other drink to serve their own houses, and to the said special barons and substantious gentlemen to send to the Lowlands and there to buy wine and aquavitae to serve their own houses.'

The Sixth Statute required that the gentlemen of the Isles send at least their eldest son, or having none, daughter, to school in the Lowlands to learn to 'speak, read and write English.'

The carrying and use of firearms was expressly forbidden under the Seventh Statute, even for the shooting of game. This must have been greeted with horror by the assembly, who were as attached to their broadswords and muskets as they were to their drink.

Curiously, the Eighth Statute banned bards from the Isles. Considering their high social standing as hereditary poets and historians in Hebridean households, this proposal must have been as unpopular as the last.

The Ninth, and final, Statute was an undertaking which bound them all to enforce the entire set of Statutes. But how effective were these measures on a people who had previously displayed little respect for the authority of the King?

The immediate effect was negligible, as history records that the Macdonalds continued to flout the law. This led to the eventual pacification of Islay by the clan which for years had remained closest to the Crown – the Campbells. By 1614, the Privy Council called on Sir John Campbell of Cawdor (or Calder) to take possession of Islay and subdue the Macdonalds once and for all. He was well placed to do so, being both powerful and rich enough to afford the rental. He took control of the island in 1615, claiming 'the forfeitures of all those in Argyll and Kintyre' and thus began an association between the Campbells and Islay which was to last until 1854.

The remaining chiefs were bound over in Edinburgh the following year to implement the Statutes, which were made tougher, if a little more realistic with regard to the carrying of arms. This they could now do, but only in the service of the King, or if hunting within a mile of their homes. However, there was a catch; their homes were to be set down in one place alone, meaning that MacLeod of Harris had to stay at Dunvegan in Skye, MacLean of Duart at Duart Castle in Mull, Clanranald at Eilean Tioram in Moidart, MacLaine of Lochbuie at Moy Castle in Mull and Gorm of Sleat at Duntuilm in Skye.

Their drinking habits hadn't changed much either, and a reduction in their household allowances was implemented. Duart, MacLeod and Gorm were all restricted to four tuns of wine a year, amounting to the not inconsiderable sum of over 1,000 gallons (4540 litres). If this seems somewhat excessive, Samuel Morewood reminded us in his exquisitely entitled book of 1838 *Inebriating Liquors*, how these quantities were consumed: *I*N

the Western Islands, many of the customs of the ancient Caledons and Britons are still preserved, and amongst others, the old manner of drinking. In former times, large companies assembled, composed principally of the chief respectable men of the islands. This assemblage was called a 'sheate', 'streah' or 'round', from the company always sitting in a circle. The cup bearer handed about the liquor in full goblets or shells, which the guests continued to drink until not a drop remained. This lasted for a day at least, and sometimes for two days, and in this practice our 'round of glasses' is supposed to have originated. During the revel, two men stood at the banquetting door with a barrow, and when any one became incapable, he was carried to his bed, and they returned to dispose of the others in the same way.

These binges were the only means available to the chiefs of relieving the unremitting gloom of the 17th Century; the present day 'ceilidh' has its roots in those intoxicating gatherings. While wine was most commonly drunk by these 'respectable men', aquavitae (or usquebaugh in Gaelic) remained the drink of the people and as such was produced on a small scale relying on the availability of grain.

For much of the first half of the 17th Century, the inhabitants, as a result of many seasons of wet weather, suffered from low yields of bere, or bigg (the indigenous strain of West coast barley). Their problems were often compounded by the common practice of paying rents with grain. Until some form of effective agrarian and social reform arrived in the Isles, distilling remained a sporadic activity designed to satisfy the needs of the local market. Aquavitae itself became a relatively precious commodity – a glut of grain often meant a burst of distilling activity which created much needed cash. Quite often distilling resulted in a shortage of grain for food, causing more problems than it solved. Islay, being the most naturally fertile island in all the Hebrides, was best placed to benefit from these gradual reforms which began to produce results in the 18th and 19th Centuries.

In the meantime, the major use for the land throughout the Isles was for the raising of stock, almost all of which found its way to the London market. The Union of the Crowns in 1603 had created a huge demand for black cattle on the London market and vast herds were moved down from the islands along the drove roads, which, largely due to the Second Statute, were serviced with change-houses. The responsibility for taking charge of cattle, sometimes representing more than half the total value of Scotland's exports to England, never weighed heavily on the minds of the hardy drovers as they slaked their thirsts at these inns. Long established sites of these change-houses can still be seen on either side of the Sound of Islay at Port Askaig and Feolin Ferry, Jura, and further up the 'Long Road' along Jura's east coast at Corran House, Lagg, and in the far north of the island at Kinuachdrach.

In 1644, the Scots Parliament levied the first excise on spirits, largely to bankroll the Royalist Army. Whether enough was raised from the 2s 8d on each Scots pint is debatable, since a great deal of distillation was still well outwith the reach of the law. The turmoil which engulfed mainland Britain during the insensitive reign of Charles I and Cromwell's Protectorate appears to have left the islands largely unaffected. The Campbells consolidated their grasp on Islay and Jura, having imported many kinsmen to act as tacksmen, taking long or indefinite leases or tacks on large grazing farms. They in turn probably had sub-tenants who, not being responsible for the rent, worked the land for no pay. This system became a considerable financial burden on the family, for only the success of the cattle droves realised the greater part of the rental payments. Poor harvests and unprofitable droves created low farm incomes, rent arrears, and often, more multiple tenancies which were extremely difficult to reverse.

Following the letter of the First Statute of Icolmkill, the Kirk's Ministers had persevered, often ineffectually, within the island parishes. A clandestine Franciscan Mission from Ireland between 1612 and 1646 had succeeded in converting some 10,000 islanders, a fact which the Protestant clergy chose to ignore and one which had moved King James to comment '. . . anybody who converts so wild a people . . . to Christianity, even if Catholicism, deserves to be thanked.'

At the end of the 17th Century Martin from Skye travelled through the Isles, observing that on Lewis the inhabitants drank:

. . . *Several sorts of liquors, as common Usquebaugh, another call'd Trestarig, id est Aquavitae, three times distill'd, which is strong and hot; a third sort is four times distill'd and this by the Natives is call'd Usquebaugh-baul, id est Usquebaugh, which at first taste affects all the Members of the Body: two spoonfuls of this last liquor is a sufficient Dose; and if any Man exceed this, it would presently stop his breath, and endanger his life.*

Colonsay, he recorded as still being a Catholic enclave, where the Protestant Minister was much resented as a burden dependent on his parishioners, taking solace in drink for 'in the presence of several gentlemen and others, after drinking of aquavitae to excess and the bottle ending sooner than he desyred, chapped on it with his hand and said the devil put the bottom out of it.' The Synod took a dim view of this as well, and threw the unfortunate man out of the Kirk.

The century closed badly for the country in general with several years of appalling harvests. Much of the population was on the brink of starvation, unable to pay the rents, which were often raised and commonly in arrears. The Union of Parliaments in 1707 effectively ended Scotland's political autonomy, leaving the future of the Hebrides very much in the hands of the lairds. Due to the long-standing tenure of the Campbells (and, no doubt strengthened by their reputation of being the King's men), Islay and Jura were exempted from direct control of the Scottish Board of Excise, and the levies remained 'in farm' to the laird. Clearly this was the simplest solution to the problem of policing a remote region, but it was far from the most efficient.

It was in Islay that the most profound influences on the distilling industry within the Isles would eventually manifest themselves; but their beginnings were to be found in the abominable conditions which prevailed in the early years of the 18th Century. In 1717, much of the livestock had perished from cattle plague, having subsisted on the corn and barley which had been put aside for the tenants who were 'next to beggary'. John Campbell, himself financially embarrassed, had just succeeded to an estate which was rapidly running downhill. Accordingly, in 1723 he agreed to a loan of £6,000 (and £500 per annum thereafter for 21 years) from one of Scotland's leading merchant financiers, 'Great' Daniel Campbell of Shawfield, MP for Glasgow Burghs, Deputy Lieutenant of Lanarkshire, and as shrewd and astute a businessman as his namesake was naive and inept. Shawfield received as security a mortgage on Islay for 21 years or until the money was repaid.

Shawfield's advantage in this deal was furthered by his own misfortune in 1725 when he voted in Parliament for an increase of 3d on a bushel of malt. This infamous Malt Tax was designed to offset a proposed excise duty of 6d on a barrel of ale, and was part of a programme to equalise duties on excisable liquors in Scotland and England, despite the fact that no mention of a tax on malt had been made in the Act of Union.

Glaswegians were incensed and vented their anger directly at Campbell, sacking Shawfield mansion in June of 1725. With customary foresight, Campbell had managed to move many valuables in time, but the damage was such that his bill of compensation from the City of Glasgow amounted to £9,000. Within a year Shawfield had managed to turn his lease into a sale of all the Campbell of Cawdor lands in Islay, including part of Jura, for £6,000 over and above the previous settlement. It is commonly believed that the purchase was due to the compensation Shawfield received after the riots.

'Great' Daniel Campbell laid the foundations which changed Islay's agricultural system from one of winter and summer grazings with common pasture land to one of larger farms supporting fewer tenants. He was particularly conscious of the fact that employment had to be created for a large number of the tenantry outwith the agricultural sector,

giving greater diversity in both jobs and services. Distilling activity appears to have remained around the croft on a small scale, since in 1722, only one-eighth of Islay's grain crop was barley, some of which would have been used to make aquavitae. However, this figure tends to confirm Thomas Pennant's observation when he visited Islay in 1772, that 'in old times the distillation was from thyme, mint, anise, and other fragrant herbs, and ale was much in use with them.'

The Malt Tax adversely affected the brewers who adulterated their ale causing a general reduction in consumption, as people turned to spirituous liquors which in the Lowlands of Scotland were largely based on cereals other than malted barley, thus avoiding the tax. Home distillers were not liable to pay excise duty, unless supplying the local market, as was probably the case in remote regions like the Isles, where the face of the Exciseman was rarely, or as in Islay's case, never seen. However, advantage was gradually taken of the greater yield of alcohol from malted barley and dutiable output increased on the

John Ramsay, distiller, Justice of the Peace, Member of Parliament and Laird of Kildalton — "a man of large intelligence and practical good sense," and one of the most progressive and humanitarian landlords of his time.

mainland. Scottish aquavitae escaped being taxed in the Gin Act of 1736, which was introduced in an effort to reduce consumption of English Gin and imported Dutch Genever; consumption of aquavitae thus doubled in 1737 to over 200,000 gallons (900,000 litres).

'Great' Daniel died in 1753, the estate passing to his grandson, Daniel the Younger on his coming of age 5 years later. Around this time aquavitae generally became accepted as a malt-derived drink, while usquebaugh was mainly the type of beverage which Pennant described. Until 1777, Daniel the Younger continued his grandfather's work as a progressive, improving laird, overseeing the development of a profitable flax industry and encouraging the mining of copper, silver and lead. Two-rowed barley as opposed to the four-rowed bere was grown to increase yields along with other crops such as turnip and clover grass, as more acreage was put to the plough. His most outstanding achievement was the creation of Bowmore in the late 1760s as the new centre of commerce for the island.

As the population of Islay increased dramatically from around 5,300 in 1753 to over 7,000 by the time the new village was constructed, new sources of employment had to be created and Campbell was quick to realise that distilling was one such source. A distillery at Bowmore was rapidly erected by David Simson, who had previously distilled in Bridgend, at the head of Loch Indaal.

Simson set the pattern for many of the commercial island distillers who followed him – all were men of diverse interests, the majority being farmers using their own barley. In this way they enjoyed a security which did not force them to depend on distilling as their sole means of income. However, Islay's position, although improved, was by no means perfect. Even after the considerable exertions of the Shawfield Campbells, it was not far removed from the situation existing throughout the rest of the Hebrides since famine and its incumbent ills were never far away. Pennant saw a great deal which

impressed him in Islay but also observed 'people worn down with poverty: their habitations scenes of misery, made of loose stones; without chimnies, without doors excepting the faggot opposed to the wind at one or other of the apertures, permitting the smoke to escape through the other, in order to prevent the pains of suffocation . . . the inmates, as may be expected, lean, withered, dusky and smoke dried.'

Famine did grip Islay and the entire nation in 1782 and a ban on distilling was made in Argyll in an effort to save grain stocks. The Government sought to reduce legal output by nearly doubling duty to 4s per gallon of spirit. Nevertheless, the public's thirst for whisky remained unquenched and dram drinking (a dram being one third of a pint of whisky containing 60% alcohol by volume) was now a popular habit, both on the mainland and in the Isles. The product of the stills was of much higher quality than the Lowland grain-based whisky, due to the traditionally small stills and weak washes. The malt whisky produced by the home distillers in the Highlands was smuggled in huge quantities into the Lowlands where it was held in great esteem. The Excise were kept extremely busy dealing with this illegal trade, which had become a thorn in the side of the legal distillers, themselves overburdened by outmoded Excise regulations.

In 1784, one of the turning points in the development of the whisky industry within the Isles occurred when the Government passed the Wash Act in an attempt to ease the restrictions on the legal trade and encourage illicit distillers to take out a licence. It proved to be unsuccessful, but was amended the following year in such a way as to allow each parish two stills of 30–40 gallons (136–181 litres) volume, operated by respectable tenants appointed

The ruined Dunyveg Castle, Islay (far right), and the rebuilt Duart Castle (right). The ferry crossing from Port Askaig to Feolin on Jura (centre right), with Caol Ila in the background. The sound of Islay from Caol Ila (top).

by their lairds, and paying a licence of £1 10s per gallon of still volume. Many such licences were taken out, even though only 250 bolls per annum of malt grown in the local parish could be used in each still.

The Act also prohibited the export of whisky from the Highlands to safeguard the interests of the large Lowland distilleries. This measure backfired since the Highland product was in such great demand in the Lowlands that smuggling continued unabated, even as the output of legal spirit nearly quadrupled in the space of 2 years. But most significantly of all, the Wash Act was the beginning of the end of home distillation. Those who made it at all in the accessible Highlands did so in quantities large enough to reap them high returns from the smugglers, while the licensed stills often consumed more than the 250 boll limit which the Act decreed – a practice which the Excise often chose to ignore. Only in the far reaches of the Highlands and Islands did the small stills gurgle away unhindered in their bothy's, the face of the gauger rarely seen and little cared for.

On Islay, where the gauger would not arrive until 1797, Bowmore distillery was well established and Duncan Campbell had just left the island after distilling at Ardmore for some time. The new laird, Walter Campbell, following his elder brother who died at the age of 40 in 1777, still faced the continuing problem of a growing population; but he relentlessly pursued his policy of agrarian reform as the Reverend John McLiesh, Minister for Kilchoman parish reported in the old Statistical Account:

. . . THE PRESENT PROP-rietor has more than doubled his rents; yet the tenantry, as well as himself, are better off than ever. They have given him, as it were, an addition to his estate, by rescuing many acres of moor and moss, from a state of nature, and bringing them to yield good crops of corn and grass. On the other hand, the proprietor has given the tenants such advantageous leases, that they have greatly bettered their circumstances as well as increased their numbers, and are enabled to live much more comfortably than formerly.

But distilling had created its own special problems within Islay, as McLiesh's colleague Archibald Robertson concluded in his Parish report for Kildalton:

WE HAVE not an excise officer in the whole island. The quantity therefore of whisky made here is very great; and the evil, that follows drinking to excess of this liquor, is very visible in this island. This is one chief cause of our great poverty; for the barley, that should support the family of the poor tenant, is sold to the brewer for 17s the boll; and the same farmer is often obliged to buy meal at 1l.3s Sterling, in order to keep his family from starving. When a brewer knows that a poor man is at a loss for money, he advances him a trifle, on condition that he makes him sure of his barley at the above price; and it is often bought by the brewers even at a lower rate; while those who are not obliged to ask for money until they deliver their barley, receive 20s or more for it. This evil, of distilling as much barley as might maintain many families, it is hoped, by some means or other, will soon be abolished. It may take some time, however, to prevent the people from drinking to excess; for bad habits are not easily overcome: but there would surely be some hopes of a gradual reformation, if spirituous liquors were not so abundant, and so easily purchased.

Robertson correctly foresaw the coming of the gauger, but underestimated his impact for when the exciseman did arrive, he was accepted by the legal trade and almost totally ignored by the illicit distillers. By 1800 the situation was so bad on the island that it was suggested troops be sent to support the Officers. They never did arrive, for local volunteers had been recruited and persuaded to 'do their duty'. The resources of the Excise were nevertheless stretched, and they had particularly bad relations with the McGilvray brothers, Archibald and Alexander, who had been outlawed since 1798 after non-appearance at trial for 'maltreating the Revenue officers'! A 20 Guinea reward was offered for information leading to their capture but to no avail.

The Stent Committee of Islay, which was a latter-day local community council consisting of the laird, his tacksmen and prominent tenants, gave vent to their feelings on the matter in March of 1801, when the minutes of their biannual meeting in Bowmore recorded their resolve to inform on illegal distillers. Perhaps not surprisingly, two of the signatories of this resolve were themselves legal distillers, David Simson of Bowmore and Donald McEachern of Bridgend who were no doubt keen to see precious grain going to the right people – and precious it was, for distilling was banned by the Government later that summer following a disastrous harvest. The ban was re-enforced the next year, so it is highly unlikely that much illicit distilling was taking place at all, due to the extreme scarcity of barley in the island.

At this time Tobermory was in the relatively fortunate position of being a busy fisheries port clearing large quantities of goods, grain and liquor while offering a number of services to passing ships. The distillery was again a small affair situated on the harbour front having been established in 1798 by the young merchant John Sinclair who went on to make a considerable fortune in the area. Even with Tobermory's privileged position, its whisky never gained the reputation or commercial success which the other island malts were to enjoy – a fact which sadly to this day remains true.

All the island distilleries supplied local needs at the end of the 18th Century, but they were influenced by any legislation which the Government were prepared to introduce to control the smuggling of high quality malt from the Highlands into the Lowlands. Increases in duty proved detrimental to the legal distillers in the Highlands and many of them returned to making whisky illegally. The Excise themselves were hindered in the execution of their duties by poor pay and inept laws which made them financially responsible for any volunteers that they might have to use. The measures, which were eventually introduced in the first three decades of the 19th Century to eradicate illegal distilling, formed the basis of the present day industry in the Isles.

The lairds held a trump card in the fight against illicit distillation for the threat of eviction was often enough to discourage the practice. In the first year of the 19th Century, 157 convictions for illegal distilling occurred on the Duke of Argyll's Tiree estates, with every tenth person being evicted. Walter Campbell's efforts on Islay were not so severe, for the distillers were rarely caught, and the practice continued to occupy the Excise Officers until at least 1850.

The legal distillers in the Isles were fortunately men of diverse means during the first 15 years of the 19th Century, for little production was possible due to a run of poor harvests and wet summers – so severe at times that even the cut peat could not dry properly. At such times, the illicit distillers did not require the attention of the Excise, for their activity must have been greatly reduced. The supply of grain remained the overriding factor in production of malt whisky within the Isles until it could be guaranteed by imports (which, until Napoleon's defeat in 1815, were limited).

The war with France had led to a severely depressed economy, which in turn resulted in reduced revenue from spirits.

*T*he old farm courtyard at Octomore (above), overlooking Port Charlotte, Islay, is still enclosed by the derelict distillery buildings which were in use until the mid-19th Century.

In 1816, the Treasury was persuaded to reduce the level of duty, and thus encourage distillers to 'go legal', helping to increase revenue at the same time. The Small Stills Act of the same year allowed the use of stills of 40 gallons (181 litres) minimum volume, even weaker washes, and abolished the 'Highland Line', finally creating a uniform geographical market in which the Highland and Lowland distillers competed equally.

The Act dramatically increased the number of distilleries in the Highlands, with a similar burst of legal activity on Islay. New distilleries sprang up at Newton and Octomore while traditional sites of distillation at Lagavulin and Ardbeg were 'invaded' by legal operators. The Jura distillery, which had started in a similar manner 6 years before, would have been none the worse for the change in regulations.

Walter Campbell died in 1816 and the estate passed to his grandson, Walter Frederick, who was to be the last Shawfield laird of Islay. He was, unfortunately, a victim of circumstance, but still managed to advance the reforms begun by his predecessors and was generous in granting advantageous leases to his tenants. The financial burdens which he inherited were eventually to be his downfall, even as Islay, and particularly the distilling industry in the island, thrived.

By 1848, another nine operations had started, of which the most famous survivor is Laphroaig. Their success was largely due to the fact that the malt produced was in such great demand on the mainland that the local markets were of a lower priority. Production was now registered in thousands and not hundreds of gallons per year, but the most critical factor in their success was the Excise Act of 1823. The Act was simple but effective, allowing the continuance of small stills, but halving duty to 2s 5d per gallon of spirits produced and sanctioning a drawback of 1s 5d per gallon if the spirit was pure malt whisky, thus offsetting the greater cost of malted barley. A licence fee of £10 was all that was required for a distiller to go legal. It was now possible for legally-produced malt whisky to taste as good, and cost less than the smuggled item.

Whereas the Illicit Distillation (Scotland) Act of 1822 was to have the greatest impact on the mainland, where heavy penalties were introduced, very few convictions were brought in Islay since the distillers were rarely caught in the act — even when the Excise had employed the Customs Cutter SS *Chichester* to make runs along the southern coast of the island. What they gained in speed, they lost in conspicuity.

By 1833, the building of Talisker distillery had been completed on the remote shore of Loch Harport in the Isle of Skye, increasing the portfolio of island distilleries which survive to this day. The inland distilleries established during Walter Frederick Campbell's lairdship on Islay were all to fail eventually — only those occupying the relatively convenient seashore sites would survive into the next century.

The estate was finally sold to the English merchant James Morrison in 1853 – the descendant of a Scots drover who, after delivering cattle to Wiltshire, married and settled there. By then the industry in the islands was almost wholly subject to the wider economic forces which prevailed throughout the industry on the mainland. Its only peculiarity was this dependence on the sea for transport of goods and produce to and from the mainland and export markets. It is very likely that many of the island distilleries would not have survived an economic disadvantage such as this were it not for the fact that, of all the distillers in Scotland, only the hardiest and most resilient managed to succeed in the islands, and as we shall see, of all the whiskies, the island malts still most perfectly reflect these qualities.

*T*he establishment of Bowmore distillery (top) around 1770 was to become a crucial factor in the town's prosperity. Islay House (bottom left), built by the Campbells of Shawfield, was recently bought by an American. The casks at Bowmore (centre left), are still racked by 'dunnage'. Bowmore's copper-topped kilns (left) provide an exotic view over Loch Indaal to Islay House.

CHAPTER TWO

THE MAKING OF MALT WHISKY

MUCH HAS BEEN WRITTEN about malt whisky, and consequently there are no real secrets as to how it is made. Although some companies zealously guard the finer details of the processes which give the whisky its unique character, it is still produced in a manner not too far removed from the basic method employed by the farmer-distillers who developed industry within the islands in the 18th Century. Islay, however, is one of the few places in Scotland where the more traditional techniques are better maintained.

Whilst many distilleries receive barley in a ready-malted form to their own specification, Ardbeg, Laphroaig and Bowmore (and Highland Park in the Orkneys) still operate floor maltings, producing a large proportion of their own malt requirements. None of the mainland distilleries barring Benriach, Balvenie, Glendronach, Glen Garioch and Springbank malt their barley in this fashion any more. Modern malting techniques can now produce malt of the highest quality more efficiently, but some of the distillery operators clearly believe that by maintaining

*I*nside one of Bowmore's kilns (left). The mechanical 'shiels' which can be seen along the base of the far wall, move along the surface, gently stirring the drying barley above the peat furnace.

links with the past the image of their whisky is enhanced whilst the quality does not diminish.

The production of malt whisky is dependent on the processes of germination and fermentation, for the barley must be awakened from being a dormant seed into an active growing plant with a supply of energy-giving sugars from which alcohol, with the aid of yeast, will ultimately be extracted. A grain of barley consists of two main parts: the embryo (from which the living plant will develop); and the endosperm, surrounded by a tough cell wall, which is the starchy food store from which the embryo draws energy during the early stages of germination.

Germination is initiated by steeping the barley for 2 days in fresh water which is periodically changed. The home distillers of the past three centuries achieved this by simply placing sacks of barley in a stream for a couple of days, but the requirements of a modern distillery normally dictate the use of large cylindrical vessels, varying in capacity from 8 tonnes at Laphroaig to the huge 25-tonne steeps at Port Ellen Maltings. Steeping causes the enzymes contained within the embryo and the cell walls surrounding the endosperm to enter it, thus helping to convert the insoluble starch granules into a more soluble sugar form, which eventually aids extraction.

MALT IN THE MAKING

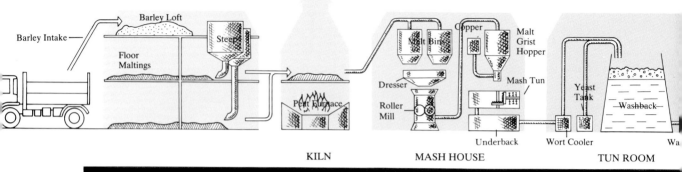

Steeping can be witnessed on Islay at Laphroaig, Bowmore and Port Ellen Maltings. The latter establishment was built in 1973 to supply Port Ellen, Caol Ila and Lagavulin distilleries with their entire malt requirements. Such large amounts require fully automated processes, in contrast to the smaller scale operations at Laphroaig and Bowmore.

The steeps at Laphroaig are loaded directly from the barley loft above the floor maltings. Four hundred tonnes of ripe, graded, Scottish barley lie in the loft and its quality is critical, for if it is too moist it will go mouldy and germinate improperly. The barley has a moisture content of around 10% prior to steeping, but when it is emptied from the conical lower section of the steep onto the malting floor this will have risen to around 45%. The barley is spread to a depth of about 4–6 inches; as germination continues the barley is raked and turned by hand to prevent the temperature of the piece exceeding an ideal 15°C.

Depending on the season, the long row of windows on either side of the floor are also used to aid temperature control as the piece is conditioned with the hand turning over a 7-day period. The barley sweetens as the endosperm becomes more sugary in nature, a process which the maltman calls 'modification'; the tell-tale signs are the internal development of seedling shoots

and the growth of rootlets, which the raking also helps to disentangle.

After steeping at Port Ellen Maltings, the barley is dropped by remote control into any of seven huge germination drums of 48 tonnes capacity each. Their size is such that they completely fill the ground floor and main body of the whole plant. As the barley lies on a perforated floor running the length of the drum, up to 17,000 cubic feet of conditioned air are passed every minute through the blanket of barley to effect perfect temperature control. To prevent the growing rootlets and shoots stitching the blanket together, the drums are turned two or three times a day – with seven drums turning simultaneously the Maltings have been known to almost flatten the National Grid system of Islay!

After 6 days in the drums, the barley is in the same condition as it is on the floor maltings at Laphroaig or Bowmore just before being loaded into the kilns. The grain is now soft and pulpy and further growth must be stopped if the sugars in the endosperm are to be conserved for fermentation. In this condition the barley is known as 'green malt' and is dried at a temperature no higher than around 70°C so as to preserve the vital enzymes which are busy converting the starch into sugar.

In the Laphroaig kilns the green malt, now with a moisture content of 40–42%, is

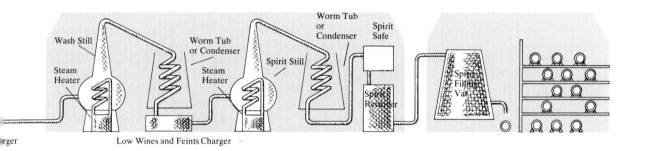

Wash Still

Steam Heater

Worm Tub or Condenser

Steam Heater

Spirit Still

Worm Tub or Condenser

Spirit Safe

Spirit Receiver

Spirit Filling Vat

rger

Low Wines and Feints Charger

STILLHOUSE

SPIRIT STORE AND WAREHOUSE

*T*he massive germination drums at Port Ellen
*(above), loaded from the steeps above, are
controlled by one operator – modern,
efficient but unfortunately underutilised.*

spread to a depth of 12 inches and hand-turned with wooden shiels· during the 2 days it stays there. Some 12 feet below the grating on which the malt lies, is the peat furnace. During kilning the constant exposure to the peat reek subtly imparts flavour to the drying malt. At Port Ellen,

kilning takes around 36 hours, but both here and at Laphroaig heavy fuel oil is consumed to generate hot air for the major part of the drying process, with peat used as a secondary fuel. In Islay whiskies, however, the peat is of great importance since these whiskes are characteristically heavier in body and flavour than their mainland cousins. The kilns at Bowmore are truly unique in that hot air is blown through the malt from below by fans using heat from a recycling system. There are also fans above the malt which help to draw the air from below so that the kilning process takes only 42 hours (compared to 48 hours at Laphroaig) and results in three full kilnings being carried out in a working week.

In the past, the home distillers achieved similar results by taking the saturated sacks of barley from the stream or bog-hole and drawing them out to drain until the grains began to germinate. It was then heaved onto a floor, and turned by hand occasionally until the shoots had grown half-way down the near transparent grains. By thickening the piece on the floor, the temperature was raised until it could be detected by hand, at which time it was thrown into a round pile or 'withering heap' for 24 hours or longer. Having been carried to a kiln the grain was dried by peat over which rotten straw and then a hair-cloth was often placed to prevent loss.

The remains of many such kilns can still be seen on Jura. Although they are officially described as lime kilns, it is almost certain that they were also employed to make malt. An example can still be seen in the nearby wood at the ruins of An Carn, but local knowledge also suggests that it could even have been used to fire an illicit still. These kilns were stone structured bodies commonly 10 feet across at the base, tapering to a height of 4 feet, where the diameter of the opening was around 6 feet. Within, the walls sloped in to a base some 3 feet wide where a small tunnel led to the site of the drying fire on the outside. It was a reasonably efficient, though relatively primitive, method when compared to the modern distillery kilns in which loss through burning is unheard of.

The malt which leaves the kiln has a moisture content of around 3–4% and is therefore noticeably firmer than green malt. It is then stored before use in the next major stages of malt whisky production, namely mashing, fermentation and finally distillation.

Both Bowmore and Laphroaig can produce about 50% of their total malt requirement in their floor maltings. The remainder arrives in bulk form from commercial maltsters in Scotland and Eire

A lime kiln in the Oa, Islay (above). Once used in the illicit production of malt, they are now more likely to contain the remains of the odd sheep which may have stumbled into them.

where it is produced in much the same way as in Port Ellen. After release from storage the malt is stripped of all dried rootlets and shoots, which conveniently find a ready market as animal feed. The malt itself is ground to a coarse grist by large mechanical roller mills, which aids sugar extraction during mashing. The ancient counterparts of these mills can be found in the rotary querns, or hand mills which were fashioned from a solid piece of stone, and remained common within the Isles until the 1860s when water-powered mills eventually predominated.

Mashing can be witnessed at any of the distilleries which are currently in production, but again there are variations on the theme to be found in the islands. The process is carried out in a large cylindrical tank (often 20 feet across) called a mashtun. The more modern covered, or roofed tuns are usually constructed of stainless steel, though Bowmore's is of resplendent copper and Bruichladdich's is iron, open-topped and over 100 years old. By peering into any of the island mashtuns, you can clearly see, about 6 feet below, a raised perforated floor made up of individual plates, sitting just clear of the bottom of the tun. The grist is poured onto this floor along with a quantity of hot water at about 65°C – the resulting brew is agitated by an arrangement of stirrers revolving around a central vertical axle. Depending on the efficiency of the mixing and extraction equipment, the capacity of the mashtun may vary.

At Jura distillery an efficient lauter tun allows two mashes of 4.75 tonnes of malt to be completed in about 9.5 hours, whereas at Laphroaig the non-lauter tun processes around 7 tonnes of malt in 10.5 hours. In both cases the tun is emptied of fluid (which is retained) and refilled three or four times with increasingly hot water to extract all the sugars from the grist.

During mashing the enzymes continue to break down the complex starch molecules into the simpler sugars; the resulting sweet liquor is called the wort. Usually, the first two waters are drained from the bottom of the tun into an underback and the final water returned to the tun as the first water of the next mash, helping to maximise the extraction of the sugars. The spent grist, left lying on top of the grating, is removed from the tun and sold as draff to the local farmers.

Fermentation is not quite the simple and phrenetic activity which it appears to be, but a series of complex chemical reactions of which the main by-product is alcohol. All this takes place within the washback, traditionally constructed of oak or pine and resembling an enormous vat sometimes 20 feet in depth. Caol Ila possesses some of the largest washbacks in Islay. They are constructed from Oregon Pine, but stainless steel is now being used more extensively. Examples of the stainless steel type can be seen at Bowmore and Laphroaig.

The wort passes through a heat exchanger to cool the fluid to around 21°C to preserve the sugars of which it is now predominantly constituted. Once this known volume of wort begins to enter the washback a small, but precise amount of living yeast is added, and fermentation commences. The yeast absorbs part of the sugars as food in the absence of oxygen, the end products being alcohol and carbon dioxide. A system of rotating arms called switchers is usually employed to control the frothing head of the brew as the reactions proceed and the carbon dioxide continues to erupt from the liquid. Fermentation is a violent, seething activity and it is not advisable to peer too closely into a washback for the lack of oxygen can literally take your breath away.

The living yeast multiplies, eventually consuming all the available sugars, and activity then dies down after some 40 hours with the resultant brew or wash containing what yeast is left, water, and around 5–6% alcohol. The wash is then checked by the distillery management to ascertain the yield of alcohol to be expected when it has been distilled.

The compounds which make up the wash all have differing boiling points. The effect of distillation upon them is to separate one from the other so that the

*T*he mashing apparatus at Laphroaig (above) has a system of rotating stirrers which ensure that the barley releases its sugars into the hot brew. The extraction of the sugars is achieved by draining the tun and adding increasingly hot waters to the grist.

desirable alcohols with lower boiling points are extracted first, thus producing spirit. To achieve this, the wash is transferred to the wash stills, which are basically onion in shape, made of copper and usually heated internally by coil tubing conveying steam. As the wash is brought to boiling point the alcohols evaporate first and rise up the neck of the still. They then pass over into the condenser, where they are cooled and liquefy, running down into a receiver called the low wines and feints charger. Gradually the proportion of alcohols within the condensate decreases as the amount of water vapour increases. When only pure water vapour is present, distillation is stopped, the product being nothing more than a dilute impure spirit containing about 15% alcohol by weight – so it must be redistilled.

The low wines are then passed into the low wines or spirit still and the process is repeated with the more volatile compounds again boiling off first – these are called the foreshots and are sent back to the low wines and feints charger. When the distillate reaches the required strength it is diverted into the spirit receiver. The

A 7-day malting floor at Laphroaig Distillery (below) where the barley is regularly handturned and raked to control germination (bottom). Cleanliness is all important, and dust, which is a fire hazard, must be removed from the barley loft whenever the steeps are not in use (right). The peat furnace at Laphroaig (far right) is much as it would have looked a century ago, when the distillery was rebuilt.

integrity of this portion of the spirit is determined by the stillman who makes a series of checks on it. These consist of the specific gravity or density, and also the reaction of the spirit to the addition of distilled water, to proof strength, to a sample. If the mixture clouds then it is impure and not collected.

These tests are all carried out within the confines of the spirit safe, a glass-walled, brass-bound case through which all the run-off from the stills must pass. The stillman can test and divert the spirit from one receiver to another by turning taps outwith the safe, but he cannot open the safe during distillation since the distillery management hold the keys to the large brass padlocks which secure it. The management submit a return to the Customs and Excise of the amounts of wash and spirit produced – a more relaxed arrangement than that which existed before April 1983 when the Customs and Excise Officer measured the yields and held the keys.

When the strength of the spirit drops back below the desired level, the remaining distillate (or feints) is diverted back to the low wines and feints charger containing the foreshots, where the resulting mixture is redistilled with the next charge of low wines. The feints consist of the heavier compounds and less volatile constituents of the low wines such as fusel oil, which although undesirable compared to the purer ethanol of the middle cut, appear (with some elements of the foreshots) in small quantities in the final product, helping to contribute to the character of each malt whisky.

The chemistry of the low wines is complex, since there are literally hundreds of compounds present, along with some which have yet to be identified. They all

Ardbeg washbacks (above left) c. 1912 with belt-driven 'switchers'. Tobermory distillery employs the common water-jacket condensers (above), while Talisker's more remote location justifies the continued use of traditional wooden worm tubs (above right).

appear, to a greater or lesser degree, in the whisky which we drink from the bottle. These compounds are collectively known as the congenerics and are responsible for the distinctive nose and flavour of the island whiskies – they help give Laphroaig that hint of seaweed for which it is famous, Bowmore that rich peaty-smoky bouquet and Jura that subtle, Highland freshness.

The home distillers and smugglers of the 18th and 19th Centuries were able to produce their whisky with equipment and utensils which have recognisable counterparts in all of the existing island distilleries, particularly Bowmore and Laphroaig.

Having ground their malt in a hand mill or with the help of an understanding local miller, they relied on a number of casks, usually of 50 gallons (230 litres) capacity, in which they prepared their mash and wash. Fermentation was started by the addition of bub, that is a small amount of barm, or yeast mixed with a little of the wort as a pre-mix and then added to the casks of wash to accelerate the onset of the process. The entire operation was carried out in a convenient farm steading, or, in the case of the illicit distillers, in seashore caves or hollows high on the bleak moors. When the Excise did trudge over the landscape in search of the distillers they almost always found the bothys unoccupied. Between May 1837 and January 1844 the Excise working out of Port Ellen seized five stills, 198 bushels of malt (only five of grain), 18 empty casks, 950 gallons of wash, four casks of low wines and one malt mill. Most

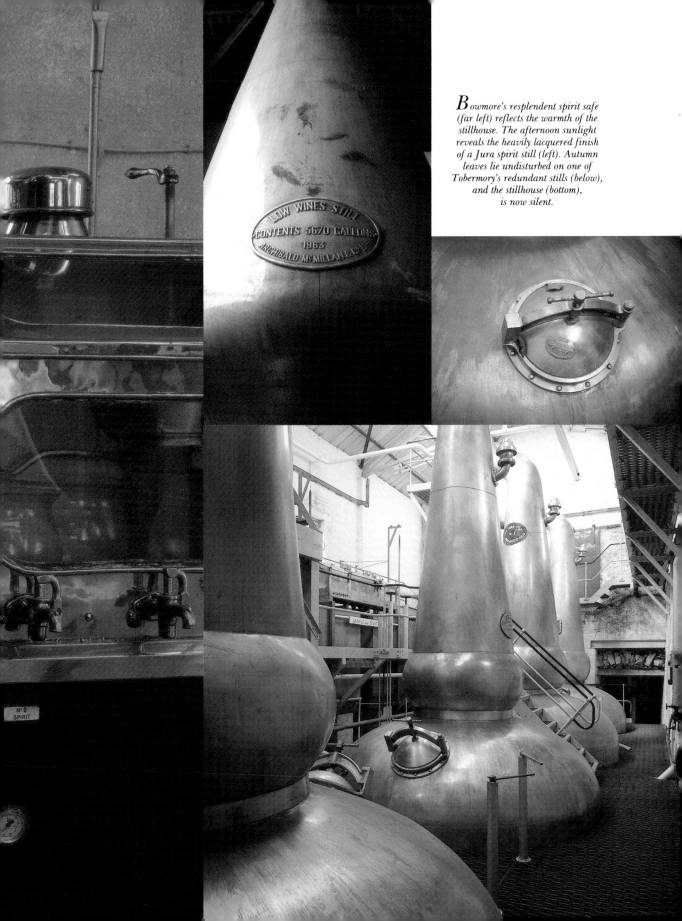

*B*owmore's resplendent spirit safe (far left) reflects the warmth of the stillhouse. The afternoon sunlight reveals the heavily lacquered finish of a Jura spirit still (left). Autumn leaves lie undisturbed on one of Tobermory's redundant stills (below), and the stillhouse (bottom), is now silent.

of this was destroyed on the spot – the Officers invariably cited that 'the items were too bulky to remove to Port Ellen'; or was it perhaps the thought of that long trek back over the moor?

Normally the distillate was cooled by running down the neck of the still and passing through a coil, or worm placed in a cask of cold water, known as the worm tub. This feature has gradually given way to the more efficient water-jacket condenser in most modern distilleries, although Talisker still employs the traditional method. However, one of the oldest tricks still employed by some distillers is the use of soap during distilling. Samuel Morewood pointed out how important this was: *I T IS A mistaken notion to suppose that soap is used only by the great distillers, since it is considered an indispensible article by every person who understands the mode of working a still on the old system.*

Why is soap used? Simply because it acts as a surfactant and reduces frothing within the still, particularly when it is directly heated by coal or gas. In contrast, the use of hub died out in the 1900s, since there was found to be more chance of inducing bacteriological infection in the pre-mix. The use of a smaller amount of living yeast has put an end to this.

What then is the destiny of the whisky prior to the bottle? It enters the receiver at about 70% alcohol by volume and is normally casked at this strength. The casks come in a number of sizes, each type having an important effect on the maturing whisky – generally, the larger the cask, the longer is the maturation time. During storage in bond various chemical reactions take place within the cask, the whisky itself changing gradually in nature. The oak wood imparts some chemical components to the whisky and these react to produce subtle changes in the spirit. The very atmosphere of the bonded warehouse can exert an effect as well, for the casks are porous and evaporation of around 1–2% of the contents per annum is allowed for by the Customs and Excise.

Within the earthen-floored vaults at Bowmore one can sense this relationship as natural moisture seeps from the soil and lies in long pools between the rows of barrels – the temperature is neither warm nor cool, the smell dank and musky. Most of these casks are of American origin, being old Bourbon casks which by law could only be used once in their native country. The law no longer stands and there has been a corresponding increase in cask prices over recent years.

Some of the cask ends carry the customs stamps and language of Spain, with 'Xerez' clearly marked into the wood. These are sherry casks, traditionally the most ideal in which to mature whisky, but sadly, due to their scarcity, now used less and less in the bonds of Scotland, although Macallan still insist on this type of cask alone. The main advantages of the sherried cask are that it is of perfect size (110 gallons or about 500 litres) and that it imparts a rich, warm colour to the whisky. They are invariably preferred to the ubiquitous pre-treated casks which were pioneered by the Glasgow whisky broker W P Lowrie in 1890. He found that by swilling out a new cask with a dark sherry and allowing the wood to soak it up, the whisky emerged resembling the sherried item. Nowadays, a concentrate called pajarete is used to this effect, but many distillers and blenders, including Charles Mackinlay who own the Jura distillery, will not pre-treat their casks in this manner.

So the whisky lies for the legal minimum of 3 years, gradually changing in character and composition until such time as it is required for bottling as a single malt, for export in bulk form, or for use in blending. All the island malts are available in bottled form, although Caol Ila and Port Ellen can only be obtained from the independent bottlers Gordon & MacPhail of Elgin. They all differ, some subtly, some not so, but they are all regarded highly and are amongst the most important malts used in blending. It is true to say that very few blended whiskies of the countless which are available in the world today do not have an island malt in their make up.

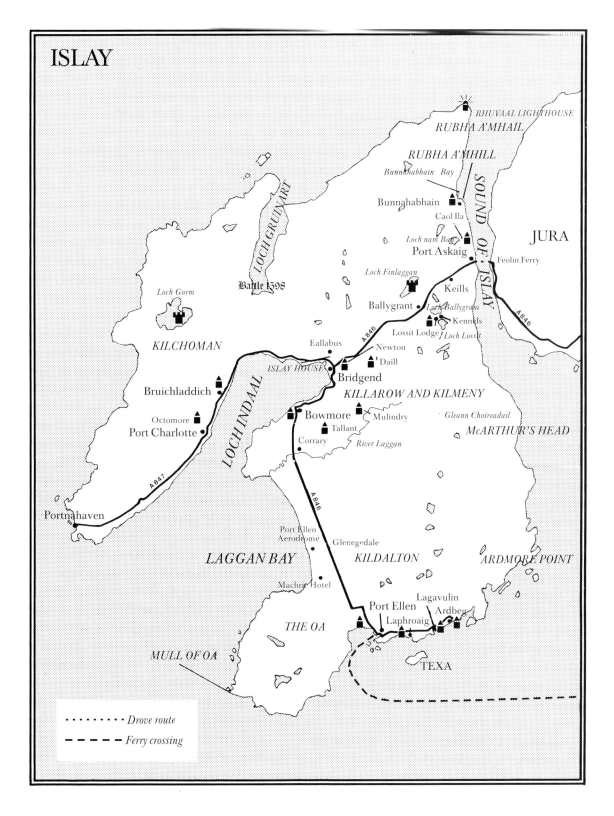

ISLAY

RHUVAAL LIGHTHOUSE
RUBHA A'MHAIL
RUBHA A'MHILL
Bunnahabhain Bay
Bunnahabhain
Caol Ila
JURA
Loch nam Ban
Port Askaig
Feolin Ferry
Loch Finlaggan
Keills
LOCH GRUINART
Battle 1598
Ballygrant
Loch Ballygrant
Kennels
Loch Gorm
Lossit Lodge
Loch Lossit
KILCHOMAN
Eallabus
Newton
ISLAY HOUSE
Daill
Bridgend
Bruichladdich
KILLAROW AND KILMENY
Octomore
Mulindry
Gleann Choireadail
Port Charlotte
Bowmore
McARTHUR'S HEAD
Tallant
Corrary
River Laggan
LOCH INDAAL
A846
Port Ellen
Aerodrome
Glenegedale
ARDMORE POINT
KILDALTON
Portnahaven
A847
LAGGAN BAY
Machrie Hotel
Lagavulin
Port Ellen
Ardbeg
Laphroaig
THE OA
MULL OF OA
TEXA

.... Drove route
– – – Ferry crossing

35

CHAPTER THREE

ISLAY

THE KILDALTON DISTILLERIES

THE DISTILLERIES OF KILDALTON all lie along a 3-mile (5-km) stretch of the A846 to the east of Port Ellen, the town established by Walter Frederick Campbell in 1821 and named after his first wife Eleanor. Port Ellen sits at the base of the neck of the land separating the peninsula of Oa from Kildalton which stretches up and around the island's south coast beyond the reach of the public road. A Caledonian MacBrayne ferry from Kennacraig arrives each day throughout the year. To disembark, ignoring the Oa, and then head down the road to Kildalton would be to miss a fascinating chapter in the history of whisky. Oa's deep inland glens and hidden caves became the source of a great deal of work for the Excise in the first half of the 19th Century.

Operating from Port Ellen the Excise Officers had the miserable job of searching out the smugglers' bothys in all weathers. They were not the hardiest of people – almost all of them came from the mainland and they regularly petitioned the Board of Excise for two weeks 'sick' leave. That the Excise almost always came across illicit distillation in the same places says as much for their enthusiasm as it does for the suitability of the terrain for the distillers.

The road to the Oa runs past the Port Ellen bonded warehouses, eventually running out at Killeyan, or Killain. At least one of the caves along the coast near Killeyan was often used for storing malt, while a little further north at Giol, more extensive operations were possible – with 8 bushels of green malt and 250 gallons (1,135 litres) of wash confiscated in one instance. On the very point of the land, at the Mull of Oa, stands the gaunt memorial to the American sailors who lost their lives in 1918 when the *Tuscania* sank off the coast. There were so many corpses washed ashore that the floor maltings in Port Ellen were used as the mortuary.

Other haunts were Cragabus and Stremnishmore. With the help of the Customs Cutter SS *Chichester*, the Excise finally caught some distillers red-handed in February 1850 in a cave near Lower Killeyan. Although they made off, they were all known faces whom the Excise later arrested. The Excise reported that they:

... WERE OBLIGED TO DESCEND over a precipice about 70 feet deep and during the time they were descending the smugglers fled by some outlet among the rocks which was not easy to discover; their names are Alexander

---

The moisture laden earthen floors at Bowmore ensure a perfect maturing atmosphere (top left). Spanish sherried oak butts (left). Prepared casks await filling at Bowmore (far left).

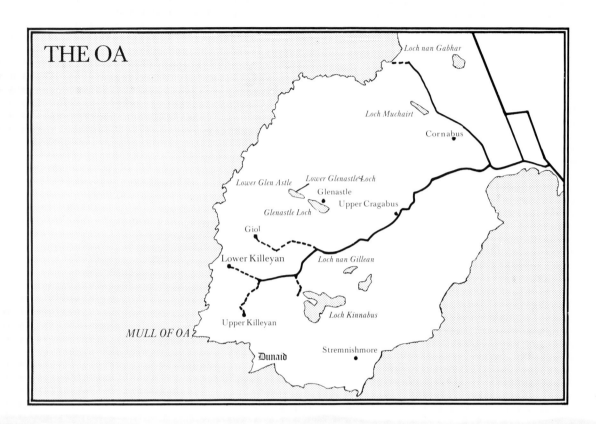

THE OA

Loch nan Gabhar

Loch Muchairt

Cornabus

Lower Glen Astle   Lower Glenastle Loch

Glenastle

Glenastle Loch   Upper Cragabus

Giol

Lower Killeyan   Loch nan Gillean

Upper Killeyan   Loch Kinnabus

MULL OF OA

Dunaid   Stremnishmore

McCuaig of Upper Killain, Donald McGibon of Lower Killain and Neil McGibon his brother. There were also in the cave five large casks containing about 300 Gallons of wash ready for distillation which they completely destroyed.

After their arrest the men made a plea, albeit unlikely, to the effect that they 'had no concern whatever with the private Distillery but mearly went into the cave by way of curiosity and they happened to be there when the Officers came but they are willing to come forward and prove against the real party concerned . . . Duncan Campbell of Giol, John McIntyre and Neil McIntyre his Brother both residing in Glenegadale Moor . . .'. It didn't work and the men, unable to pay a steep £30 fine each, were jailed at Inveraray for 3 months, despite the magnanimity of the Excise in asking for clemency due to their extreme poverty.

Safe anchorages and better access by road and sea led to the successful distillers consolidating themselves on the other side of Port Ellen. Although the coast is exposed to the south-east, shipping has never been so hindered by poor weather as to prevent production. For years supply boats have made their way into the relatively sheltered anchorages at Ardbeg, Lagavulin, Laphroaig and Port Ellen itself. Even today it is still possible to follow the routes taken by the vessels from Islay up to Skye.

The approach to Lagavulin is dominated by the impressive outline of Dunyveg Castle. It must have been a formidable prospect for the enemies of the Macdonalds and even now the ruins dwarf any passing boats.

The coast road runs past all the Kildalton distilleries and at its easterly limit lies Tallant. One is tempted to think that this is where the ubiquitous Johnstons distilled for the best part of a century, but they were at the other Tallant on the far side of the Laggan Bog. It seems that the last John Johnston to operate there never did so on a profitable commercial scale and he was described by the Excise in 1838 as being in 'very low circumstances'. Frequently

Tallant Farm, by Bowmore.

reported to the Board of Excise for undue reductions in stock, he seems to have been generous with his drams for visiting workmen ('. . . generally great dram drinkers . . .') and small farmers bringing grain 'for sale' around New Year when as much as 2 gallons of malt were once consumed!

This may have been one of the reasons why Johnston was soon in '. . . embarrassed circumstances . . .', but with an output of only 220 gallons (1,000 litres) a week, he was never a match for the bigger and better situated distilleries along the Kildalton coast. Although his business folded around 1852, his brother Donald and his son Alexander were to be successful distillers figuring prominently in Laphroaig's development. At Tallant in Kildalton, however, there was an exceptional smithy thanks to the local bog water it used for tempering.

Between Tallant and the shore the famous Kildalton Cross stands within the cemetery where John Campbell, one of the descendants of Duncan Campbell of Ardmore was returned for burial from Mull in the 1860s where he had been Chamberlain to the Duke of Argyll

*C*las Uig, Islay (above). The landing point for Chamberlain John Campbell's burial party from Mull can be seen clearly beyond the Alystra's anchorage.

The circumstances surrounding the funeral are worth retelling, since they display how different versions of a perfectly straightforward local event can arise from nothing more than a desire to tell a good yarn. Campbell's body was brought down from Mull by steamer to the tiny bay of Clas Uig beyond Ardmore Point, where the coffin was unloaded and carried up the rough hillside by the local gentlemen, mostly Campbells and Mac-Neills. Provisions were also brought from Mull for all the mourners, so that a banquet could be held before the boat returned.

But after the passage of many years, a local version of the funeral slowly emerged which incorrectly claimed that Campbell's body had arrived in Port Ellen, to be borne down the coast road by a relay of villagers along the route. The length of the journey, and the burden of the coffin necessitated 'wee rests' along the way which were made doubly pleasurable by some justifiable dram-drinking.

The unfortunate outcome of this, so the story goes, is that when the villagers finally arrived at the graveside, they found that they no longer had the coffin. It is claimed that on retracing their steps they came upon the solitary coffin lying by the roadside just up the brae from Surnaig House at Lagavulin. This is undoubtedly a fabrication, but its retelling is none the worse for it.

A more factual, but equally interesting tale involving the Campbells arose when the old family home at Ardmore was converted into a barn after the building of the new house in 1873. Being descended from one such as Duncan Campbell, the entire family was extremely musical and they were all renowned fiddlers. On raising the wooden floor to replace it with newly-invented concrete, a remarkable sight was beheld – the entire floor-space was filled with clean cattle skulls. Any macabre conclusions that arose were dashed when it was explained that Duncan Campbell had placed them there in the belief that the skulls made the floor a better sounding board!

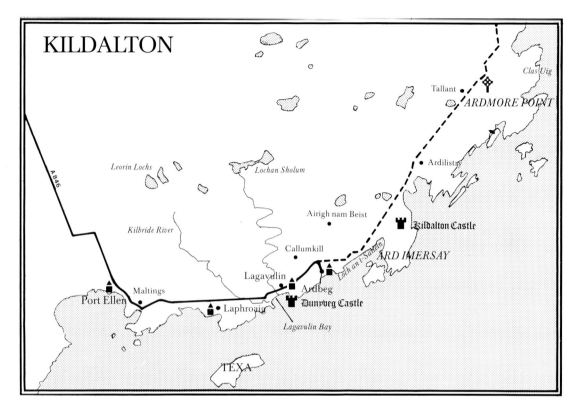

KILDALTON

ARDBEG

Not until 1977, when the Canadian company Hiram Walker & Sons finally gained control of Ardbeg was the long family connection with the MacDougalls finally severed. Since 1798 the family had resided as farmers and distillers in the area, being tenants in Ardbeg, Airigh nam Beist and half of Lagavulin farms. Distilling operations had been going on in the area prior to the sequestration of Alexander Stewart in 1794, but were not restarted on a commercial basis until 1815 by Duncan MacDougall's son John. In 1886, when Alfred Barnard was collecting information for his book *The Whisky Distilleries of the United Kingdom* for Harper's Gazette of London, he reported that by 1835 output was around 500 gallons (2,270 litres) a year.

The financial backing for the distillery appears to have come from the Glasgow merchant Thomas Buchanan Jnr, for in 1838 Walter Frederick Campbell granted a lease for the Ardbeg farm with 2 acres to Buchanan for 57 years and disposed of the distillery for £1,800. John's son Alexander had by then taken over the distilling operations, and leased the farm at Airigh nam Beist for a yearly rental of £45, trading as Alexander MacDougall & Co. Alexander appears to have been a character as Barnard recalls: *...HIS CLAN-nishness was intense. This Highland virtue he prominently exhibited on a certain occasion, when he discovered in court that some unknown namesake was pronounced by the judge 'Guilty' and sentence of a fine or imprisonment was imposed, Mr McDougall interposed the statement 'that it was impossible that a McDougall could do anything wrong' and therefore he would pay the fine!*

Some of his employees were not so generous towards him, for he spent the latter part of his adult life confined to a wheelchair and, according to the Excise, was therefore 'more easily imposed upon by his servants.' The disability led to his sister Margaret joining her brother as a licensee, and handing over management of the distillery to Colin Hay, the son of Walter Frederick Campbell's coachman, some 3 years before Alexander died in 1853. Margaret and her sister Flora then acquired lets 'of the farms of Ardbeg and half Lagavulin' in 1851 from James Brown, Trustee for the sequestered estate of Walter Frederick Campbell. The lease clearly states that the sisters were 'Co-Partners carrying business at Ardbeg as Distillers under the firm of Alexander MacDougall & Co . . .'. Despite Colin Hay's presence they may well have been Scotland's first lady distillers, but the true extent of their involvement in the distillery proper can only be surmised, suffice to say that Margaret was 63 when she was granted the lease!

Under Hay, Ardbeg grew into a small community based around the distillery – in 1853, he estimated that there were some 200 people living there. He became sole proprietor after the deaths of the Mac Dougall sisters but trained one of his two sons, Colin Elliot as a distiller while backing still came from the Buchanans. His other son Walter became a doctor and remained a partner in the distillery. At the time of Barnard's visit in 1886 the inventory included a 16-feet diameter cast iron mashtun some 5½ feet in depth, eight washbacks of 8,000 gallons (36,320 litres) each, one wash still of 4,000 gallons (18,160 litres) and one spirit still of 3,000 gallons (1,362 litres) producing a then prodigious 250,000 gallons (1.135 million litres) per year with a workforce of 60 people.

By 1888, a new lease was granted to Alexander Wilson Gray Buchanan (heir to Thomas Buchanan Jnr), and Colin Elliot Hay which included rights to the Ardbeg pier costing £100 per year. Four years into the lease Colin Hay was forced to write to Peter Reid, the Ramsay's factor at Port Ellen, claiming that this was 'a very heavy charge in these times of diminished trade . . . It amounts to 7½d per ton on all the goods brought in and sent out by us', implying that some 3,200 tons of barley,

ARDBEG DISTILLERY
BY PORT ELLEN, ISLAY, ARGYLL

Owners:
HIRAM WALKER & SONS (SCOTLAND) PLC
3 HIGH STREET, DUMBARTON G82 1ND

Licensees:
ARDBEG DISTILLERY LTD

Manager:
MR D RAITT
Telephone: 0496 2244

Arbeg's current shutdown is evident as soon as the distillery is approached from the main road. A silence hangs over the plant which lacks the peat reek and stench of fermentation that so easily identify a working distillery. Scaffolding sprouts peculiarly from one of the pagoda roofs of a malt kiln, betraying the fact that only maintenance work is now being carried out.

ESTABLISHED 1815

Ardbeg

FINEST
ISLAY SINGLE MALT
SCOTCH WHISKY

Guaranteed 10 years old

ARDBEG DISTILLERY LIMITED
ISLE OF ISLAY ARGYLL SCOTLAND

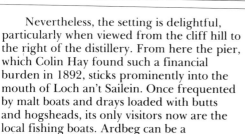

The Clydesdale *(left) takes on casks at Ardbeg pier at the turn of the century. Pagoda roofs at Ardbeg Distillery undergoing renovation (below).*

Nevertheless, the setting is delightful, particularly when viewed from the cliff hill to the right of the distillery. From here the pier, which Colin Hay found such a financial burden in 1892, sticks prominently into the mouth of Loch an't Sailein. Once frequented by malt boats and drays loaded with butts and hogsheads, its only visitors now are the local fishing boats. Ardbeg can be a depressing place to begin a tour of the distilleries of Islay, but it is a very real reminder of the precarious state of the industry at present. A happier picture begins to emerge down the coast at Lagavulin, a 20-minute walk along the road.

casks, whisky and sundries were passing up and down the pier each year.

Colin Hay had ceased active farming at Ardilestry in 1889, having lived closer to the distillery for a number of years until the end of the century when he died on February 10th 1899. The community nature of Ardbeg at that time is obvious from the terms of the new lease which was granted in 1900 to Hay's sons for '. . . All and whole the Distillery of Ardbeg. . . also the farm of Ardbeg. . . excepting from the said farm the School and Teacher's house of Ardbeg . . .' which had been instigated by the laird John Ramsay's first wife, Eliza, and completed after her death in 1864.

In 1902 the firm was incorporated as a limited company which was to purchase Ardbeg from Captain Iain Ramsay in 1922, becoming the third of the Kildalton distilleries which he was forced to sell to maintain his despressed estate. The sum of £19,000 saw the distillery and its land change hands with £9,000 being paid as cash with interest at 5% per annum from Whitsun 1922, and £10,000 being secured in the form of a Bond and Disposition to be reduced to £5,000 by 1927, and finally written off by 1932. Such were the economics of the Depression. Thus Alexander MacDougall & Co continued to manage Ardbeg until its liquidation in 1959 when Ardbeg Distillery Ltd was formed, being superseded in 1973 by the Ardbeg Distillery Trust comprising the Distillers Company Limited (DCL) and Hiram Walker & Sons Ltd.

Ardbeg has always been Islay's dark horse, considered by many locals as variable, but when good, very good indeed. A traditional distillery in such a situation as Ardbeg, with an output, almost all of which went for blending, would obviously have struggled to survive the economic strictures of the 1970s and when Hiram Walker finally acquired full control of the company in 1977, only 5 years of production were enjoyed before being stopped with the loss of 18 jobs. This more or less finished Ardbeg as a normal community.

That this fate should befall such a remote community which was centred around the distillery is particularly sad. Don Raitt, the manager, could only parry the question of re-opening with the heartfelt comment, 'Well, we are spending money on the place.' The maintenance helps to give a semblance of normality, but only when the stills are fired once more will Ardbeg begin to resemble the place it once was.

LAGAVULIN

Lagavulin can lay claim to being one of the oldest distilleries in Scotland – it is almost certainly built on the oldest site of established distilling activity on Islay. Barnard was informed when he passed through that around 1742 there were 'ten small and separate smuggling bothys for the manufacture of "moonlight", which when working presented anything but a true picture of "still life", and were all subsequently absorbed into one establishment, the whole work not making more than a few thousand gallons per annum.'

Firm evidence of this appears in an inventory taken in June 1784 of the belongings of Duncan Campbell of Ardmore, who had been the tacksman for the Miln farm and half of Lagavulin.

Campbell, whose family had been Chamberlains to Campbell of Cawdor in Kildalton, is reputed to have got into difficulties following the ban on distilling on Islay in 1783 and the introduction of the Wash Act the next year. He fled the island and being something of a bard, a romantic legend persists today, recalling that as he rowed from Islay's southern shore he sang his 'Praise of Islay':

See afar yon hill Ardmore,
Beating billows wash its shore;
But its beauties bloom no more
For me now far from Islay.

Ardbeg Distillery (top), a thriving community last century, supporting a population in the hundreds, now lies silent. Maintenance work on the pagoda-roofed kilns continues (right and far right) and a healthy water supply (above right) is well in evidence.

His tack was assigned to the laird, Walter Campbell and his belongings disposed of by Malcolm MacNeil of Ardtallay.

John Johnston of the Tallant distilling family, had meanwhile taken a lease on the other half of the Lagavulin farm, with the approval of Godfrey MacNeil, the tacksman for Callum Kill, and holder of a great many other tacks in Kildalton. MacNeil was well disposed to the family for his daughter Elizabeth had married a Johnston from Corrary, where just across the River Laggan at Island, the MacNeils had their fishing lodge.

Johnston maintained some degree of distilling activity at Lagavulin until 1835 – his two sons Donald and John were farmer-distillers at Laphroaig and Tallant respectively. Johnston died in 1836 and was followed in December of that year by Alexander Graham, a Glasgow distiller-merchant and owner of the Islay Cellar, which supplied Islay malts in Glasgow. It seems that Johnston had got into debt with Graham to the extent that Graham was named as his executor creditor. Graham was no stranger to Islay in any case. His wife, Eleanor, was the daughter of Dr Samuel Crawford, the surgeon and resident factor to the laird. Crawford's wife Margaret was the daughter of James Campbell of Ballnaby whose land had been originally held by the Beatons, the surgeons to the Lords of the Isles, and was never a part of the Islay Estate.

A valuation carried out in 1837 by Donald MacDougall clearly shows that two distilleries had been operating at Lagavulin during Johnston's tenancy. 'The Still House (No 2), Tun Room and Malt Barn No 4', were all listed as belonging to the laird Walter Frederick Campbell, as the Ardmore Distillery. The valuation for Lagavulin distillery itself was £1,103 9s 8d, excluding the farm.

Graham was granted a new lease for the distillery and farm in 1837 for 19 years, but he had no intention of remaining at Lagavulin which he merely saw as a good business opportunity for his sons, Walter and John Crawford Graham. Walter did the distilling until 1848, when Donald

Johnston of Laphroaig died. His Trustees than asked if he would supervise at Laphroaig until Donald's son, Dugald Johnston, was old enough to take over. He did this until November 1855, when he re-entered Lagavulin. After Alexander Graham's death in 1850, John Crawford Graham divided his interests between Lagavulin and the Islay Cellar. His Glasgow business contacts led him to meet the man who was to become his next partner at Lagavulin, James Logan Mackie.

In February 1861, a lease was granted by John Ramsay to the new partners for 5 years at a rent of £200 for the first year,

*C*aptain Iain Ramsay finally took over the Kildalton Estate, at the age of 27, after the death of his father in 1892 and his mother, Lucy, in 1905. He was forced to sell all his distilleries – Ardbeg, Lagavulin, Laphroaig and Port Ellen, in order to maintain his dwindling estate.

and £235 per annum for the remainder. At the same time, all the parties agreed to a valuation of the distillery and farm to satisfy themselves as to the extent of their mutual liabilities. This was to become the source of some friction between Ramsay and the Grahams. The survey was carried out by Edward Stewart (Ramsay's nominee) of 364 Argyle St, Glasgow, and Donald MacDougall (nominated by Walter, John Crawford and their sister Horatia Perry Graham) of Colonsay on July 15th and 16th, 1861. Curiously, the parties did not sign an agreement to the valuation until a few days later. The survey was carried out in two parts, the first dealt with the distillery and the second with the farm, dykes and boundaries. MacDougall had to return to Colonsay after the first survey, leaving Stewart to complete the valuation with the help of a Duncan MacDougall of Port Ellen, a joiner by trade, and sometime employee of John Ramsay. The figures were worked out in Ramsay's estate office, and were then submitted on unstamped paper.

Nothing was said until the valuation was given to the Graham's solicitor, Mr Faulds, who immediately raised questions. Not only was the distillery valued some £200 less than it had been in 1837, but the Grahams were also found to be owing John Ramsay £330. Faulds then employed an architect, William Spence, whose independent survey of Lagavulin amounted to £1,144. The Grahams remained generally unhappy with the circumstances surrounding the survey, to the point where they felt the presence of Ramsay's joiner MacDougall had been prejudicial. In fact they would have had difficulty casting aspersions on MacDougall's character for he was a devout Christian who once said of a Minister on probation after the death of Rev MacTavish, and who had just delivered a sermon in Kildalton Kirk, '. . . it did not appear to me as if he felt that he was in the presence of the Almighty.'

Ramsay decided to take Counsel's Opinion in 1862, stating that the Grahams had made additions to the farm without the consent of the laird, and that the distillery buildings had also been 'lessened in number'. The Grahams had indeed made alterations, but it would have been well nigh impossible for the laird to have remained ignorant of the extent of the alterations. Lagavulin was then one of Islay's largest distilleries having three malthouses and two kilns which, along with new roads and access, the Grahams had built in 1849. When the corn mill burnt down, they rebuilt it with an undertaking that the estate should pay for the timber and slate – a common enough arrangement in those days. 'In fact Mr Graham and his successors,' claimed Faulds, 'always considered the sums so expended as a fund which to a great extent would be recovered at the expiry of the lease.'

Whether a settlement was ever reached is not recorded. The dispute probably fizzled out as John Crawford Graham got down to business in his new partnership and Horatia moved to the mainland with her husband. Records of Walter Graham's whereabouts also became scarce after 1864.

Relations between Ramsay, Graham and Mackie normalised to the extent that new leases were granted over the course of the next 28 years until Mackie's nephew Peter Jeffrey Mackie, who had trained as a distiller at Lagavulin, took over as sole partner in 1889. Just after this date, 'White Horse' was launched by Mackie & Co as a brand which was to enjoy considerable success at home and abroad.

John Ramsay's son Iain maintained a good personal relationship with Mackie. Both were men of means, but this never stopped them from trying to force the other's hand when business was being conducted, habitually haggling over some minor clause in a lease. By 1902, Mackie was in partnership with Andrew Hair Holm securing the lease of Lagavulin for £800 per annum (an increase of £110 over the 1889 lease) for 50 years.

Despite the success of 'White Horse', Lagavulin was never entirely divorced from the effects of local disputes. Mackie had, until 1907, held the sales agency of Laphroaig, but suddenly lost it apparently due to an argument concerning the water

rights to the Surnaig burn, which had been secured for Lagavulin for some years, and had also been a bone of contention between Dugald Johnston and Walter Graham in 1858. Mackie reacted in characteristic style by deciding to make his own Laphroaig type whisky, and built a traditional small pot still distillery within the Lagavulin complex. The product of the Malt Mill Distillery did not really do justice to Laphroaig, which should have come as no surprise to Mackie who must have realised that Laphroaig's water had always been drawn from a bog.

Lagavulin was one of the distilleries Iain Ramsay was forced to sell off in the early 1920s, although the deal was not entirely straightforward. There were misunderstandings over the sale of the peat lands, which were transferred from the Kildalton Deer Park to the bog just south of Machrie, entailing an increased mileage over which the irascible Mackie argued. Mackie (by then Sir Peter) was very keen to gain more land than Ramsay thought necessary to secure the water rights from the Solan Lochs. Iain Ramsay insisted that water rights should extend from source to distillery with a margin of land on either side of the burn, but Mackie characteristically haggled for more than he needed. On top of this, some of the correspondence affecting the sale took time to catch up with Mackie during his not infrequent shooting trips in Scotland. The two men agreed to a sum of £16,000 for the distillery, farm, 100 acres of peat lands and the water rights.

Under Sir Peter Mackie, his company had acquired Craigellachie distillery in 1915, but after his death in 1924 the group's name was changed to White Horse Distillers Ltd, taking full advantage of the popularity of its leading brand. The massive amalgamations of the late 1920s saw the company become part of the DCL combine with Lagavulin finally coming under control of the current owners, Scottish Malt Distillers (SMD), in 1930.

Only obligatory closures due to war have marred an otherwise continuous production record to the present day, due in no small way to the outstanding quality of Lagavulin as a single malt. The common feature of rationalisation throughout the industry (which is always more evident when carried out by a company the size of DCL) has had its way at Lagavulin. Port Ellen Maltings made the floor maltings redundant in 1974 and the 'old' Malt Mill distillery finally succumbed to the economics of the 20th Century and was dismantled in 1962. For the next 7 years its quaint, coal-fired stills made whisky within the Lagavulin stillhouse to increase output. Finally, they were retired in 1969, and replaced with a pair of traditional Lagavulin pattern stills, all four being converted to internal steam heating at the same time. The old Malt Mill building is now Lagavulin's reception centre.

After the boom period of the 1970s Lagavulin escaped the SMD closures of 1983, but four jobs were lost out of a workforce of 20 and a 4-day week has been in operation for some time. The most worrying blow to 'White Horse' came in August 1984 when the DCL announced that they intended closing two bottling plants, both in Scotland – 700 jobs at the VAT 69 plant at South Queensferry and at 'White Horse', Glasgow, were to be lost with no immediate prospects of a backdown by the DCL. For many years the saving grace of the malt distilleries has been the small scale of their operation compared to the huge Lowland grain distilleries which reaped the rewards of Scotch whisky's phenomenal success, and now have to suffer as the market for blended Scotch shrinks. The world's palate is demanding something different from whisky and is fortunately just discovering what generations of Islaymen have always known, that malt whisky is like nothing else on earth. Lagavulin can be thanked and thankful for that.

The Macdonalds' ancient fortress of Dunyveg (top). Two rotary quern stones saved from the old Malt Mill Distillery welcome the visitor to Lagavulin (far left). Duncan Campbell of Ardmore's inventory of 1784 (left) which clearly shows his farming and distilling interests.

LAGAVULIN DISTILLERY
BY PORT ELLEN, ISLAY, ARGYLL

Owners:
SCOTTISH MALT DISTILLERS LTD

TRINITY RD ELGIN
MORAYSHIRE IV30 1UF

Licensees:
WHITE HORSE DISTILLERS LTD

99 BORRON ST
GLASGOW G4 9XF

Manager:
ALASTAIR ROBERTSON
Telephone:0496 2250

(Visits should be arranged through SMD at
the Elgin office. Telephone: 0343 7891)

Lagavulin Bay (above).

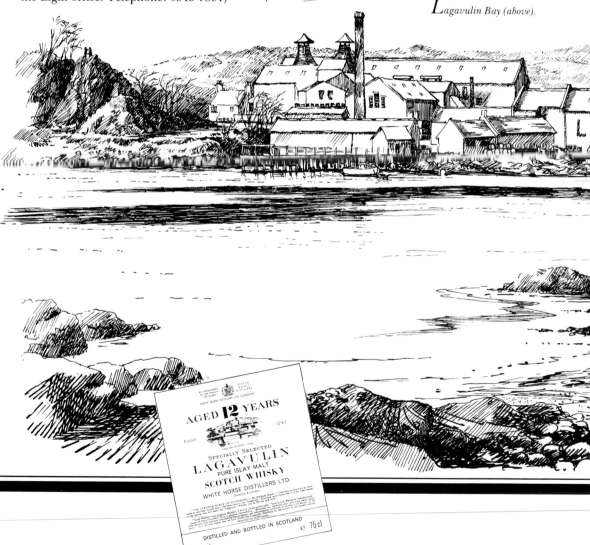

No distillery could be found amidst a more historical setting than Lagavulin which lies in a fine natural harbour with a clear view of Dunyveg Castle at the entrance. From here 1,000 Islaymen set sail to fight alongside Robert the Bruce at Bannockburn in 1314, and in this bay the Macdonalds maintained their power base as Lords of the Isles until finally driven out by the Campbells three centuries later.

Fortunately the floor maltings escaped demolition in the early 1970s when the final piece was turned, but as yet no new purpose has been found for them. The exterior of the distillery presents a crisp, clean appearance with red pagoda kiln roofs and a large glass-fronted stillhouse (a feature common to many DCL distilleries) overlooking the path down to the pier.

Just past the stillhouse a grey stone slab attached to the side of a building stands as a memorial to Angus Johnston, who died in 1830 at Lagavulin. Superstitious boatmen had refused to take the headstone across to Johnston's resting place on Texa island. One of the smaller buildings in the centre of the complex houses a reception centre for visitors who are often quite thirsty by the time they reach it. This was the old Malt Mill Distillery, and the size of the interior gives a good indication of how traditional an operation Peter Mackie had set up here. In some ways it is regrettable that the old distillery was dismantled, since the workings of it would be a joy to witness – one which would doubtless increase the number of visitors to Lagavulin.

A dram of Lagavulin is always offered by the manager, Mr Robertson – an exceptional dram at that and one which is gradually gaining acceptance with some of the other island malts as something to savour before a good meal. After that, the walk around the bay to Dunyveg Castle is doubly pleasurable. Casting an eye over the precipitous walls to the waters below it is not difficult to imagine the bay as it must have been when the Macdonalds' 'little ships' crowded it and thus gave the castle its name.

Lobster boats now come and go freely, but since the instigation of the roll on/roll off ferries to Islay in 1974, the DCL puffer *Pibroch* has been a stranger to the place.

Over the best part of 50 years there have been two *Pibroch*s working around the Hebrides. The first coal-fired boat was used by the DCL to service the SMD distilleries in Islay with the occasional summer run up to Talisker in Skye. She became something of a celebrity in 1937 when, within the space of two months, she saved the lives of 22 Fleetwood trawlermen from the *San Sebastian* and *Luneda* which had both come to grief on the treacherous rocks off Islay's southern coast. Not surprisingly she was thereafter known affectionately as the 'Fleetwood Lifeboat'.

By the late 1950s a new boat was required with more efficient diesel power so in 1957 Scott & Sons of Bowling were commissioned to construct a vessel from plans of G & G Hamilton's *Glen Shira* which had been built the previous year. Her coal-fired predecessor was renamed *Texa* and later *Cumbrae Lass* before being broken up in 1967.

The new vessel plied between Glasgow and Islay until 1974 when the introduction of roll on/roll off ferries made her redundant. A normal week's work for the skipper and crew of five involved taking around 100 tons of malt and grain to Islay, returning with about 350 hogsheads of malt whisky.

In September 1974, the *Pibroch* was purchased by Glenlight Shipping Co of Glasgow and remained in service until 1983 when she was laid up at Yorkhill Quay due to lack of sufficient work. Latterly she had been used as a tender to the US Navy in the Firth of Clyde.

The future looked a little bleak for the *Pibroch* but rumours of her impending sale brought enquiries from the United States and Japan – however, Glenlight had no intention of selling their famed asset. Finally, in February 1985 fortune smiled on the puffer when one of the Glenlight's other boats broke down on the way to the Isle of Man, requiring major engine repairs. The *Pibroch* was hurriedly recommissioned and was once more sailing to the Western Isles, back on her home ground.

*T*he Pibroch, *owned by Glenlight Shipping, passes Bunnahabhain once more; but this time her cargo is coal.*

LAPHROAIG AND ARDENISTIEL

If the MacDougalls spring to mind when Ardbeg is mentioned, then it is the Johnston family which plays the central role in Laphroaig's establishment and history. Traditionally distillers from Tallant, they were already represented at Lagavulin by John Johnston when his son Donald set up in Laphroaig around 1826 on ground belonging to the Torradale croft which was occupied by his cousin, yet another Johnston. Within 10 years Laphroaig was joined by another distillery on part of the Ardenistiel farm tack leased from Walter Frederick Campbell by James and Andrew Gairdner in 1835. The Gairdners acted as financiers and put the Ardenistiel distillery (it was also referred to as the 'Islay' and 'Kildalton' distillery) in the capable hands of James and Andrew Stein of the noted Clackmannan distilling family. The two concerns existed side by side and initially did not appear to suffer from their proximity.

In 1846 Andrew Stein died of fever, which is now thought to have been malarial in nature, and his brother moved to Port Ellen distillery to act as manager and factor to his cousin John Ramsay, having married John's sister Margaret. Ardenistiel was then assigned by the Gairdners in 1847 to John Morrison, who had been an unsuccessful manager in his stay at Port Ellen between 1826 and 1833, but was effectively being given a second chance. In June 1847, Donald Johnston died, popularly believed to have drowned in a vat of his own burnt ale. This is not quite as pleasant a way to die as one might first think. In April of the following year an Excise officer at Port Ellen distillery fell into a tank of spent wash immersing himself 'in the boiling liquor to the upper part of both thighs and was so severely scalded as to baffle every medical attention to save his life.'

Donald's eldest son Dugald, then in his minority, became heir to Laphroaig. Donald's trustees were named as Peter

The Warlight, *built in 1919 for Ross and Marshall (now part of Glenlight Shipping) offloads at Laphroaig. Sadly these coal-fired puffers have now disappeared from the West Coast of Scotland.*

MacIntyre, tenant in Ballynaughtonmore farm and John Johnston of Tallant, Donald's brother. Both men recognised the need for a knowledgeable distiller to take over the day-to-day running of Laphroaig. They installed Walter Graham (who had followed Donald's father in 1836 as distiller at Lagavulin) soon after Donald's death and also renegotiated the lease with the new laird, James Morrison in February 1854.

After James Stein withdrew from Ardenistiel, John Morrison had once more been unable to make a go of it, and he signed it over to William Hunter and John Ferguson Sharpe in 1848. He continued, however, to hold the licence and distil there until May 1851, when the Excise noted thankfully that 'Mr Morrison has paid up all his Excise duties long ago and does not intend to take out another licence.'

It seems that Morrison was never destined to be a distiller – when James Morrison visited Ardenistiel in 1848 prior to his purchase of Islay, he discovered that his namesake had 2,000 pigs grazing on Texa island!

Typically, John Morrison had responded somewhat too enthusiastically to a brilliant suggestion by Walter Frederick Campbell that pigs might be raised on the distillery farms and fed on draff. The hams could then be smoked in the kilns during the silent season and despatched by sea to the mainland. Sadly, his own bankruptcy and the advent of the railway system on the mainland put paid to Campbell's inspiration.

By the end of 1852, Hunter and Sharpe realised they had backed the wrong horse and assigned 'all and whole of the said distillery called the Kildalton Distillery . . . and the right of water from the Surnaig Burn . . .' to Robert Salmond, manager of the City and Glasgow Bank. John Morrison had by now returned to Glasgow and is recorded as being in the Glenpatrick Distillery in the 1860s, where, predictably, he was to be finally bankrupted.

The new laird of Kildalton, John Ramsay was becoming increasingly

The Johnstons of Tallant and Laphroaig

Showing how the ownership of Laphroaig moved from the Laphroaig branch of the Johnstons to the Tallant branch following the death of Dugald Johnston and the marriage of Alexander Johnston of Tallant to Isabella Johnston his cousin and the transferral of the lease to Alexander's sisters Catherine and Isabella and his nephew John Johnston Hunter Johnston.

John Johnston of Tallant and Lagavulin d.1836

Donald Johnston of Laphroaig d.1847 — John Johnston of Tallant

Dugald d.1877 — Mary — Alexander Campbell — Isabella d. circa 1905 — Alexander Johnston of Tallant d.1907 — Margaret (m.Campbell) — Ann (m Brandon)

Isabella

Isabella 1843-1927 — William Stevenson Hunter 1848-1919 — Alexander m. Isabella Johnston of Laphroaig — Catherine 1846-1926 — ? — John Johnston Hunter Johnston

Ian William Hunter d 1954

ISLAY MIST
75cl   40% Vol
THE GREAT SEAL OF ISLAY
the unique blend of
SCOTCH WHISKY
DISTILLED, BLENDED & BOTTLED IN SCOTLAND
D. Johnston & Co., (Laphroaig) Ltd., Isle of Islay, Scotland

'Islay Mist', created for Lord Margadale's coming of age in 1928.

impatient with the way things were going at Ardenistiel, but decided to give one last chance to William and Andrew Hunter, granting a lease in their favour in 1859 for 19 years.

In 1858 Dugald Johnston was assigned the land lease of Laphroaig by his father's Trustees, and Walter Graham claimed to have 'nearly doubled the capabilities of Laphroaig distillery since 1848.' Dugald Johnston gradually became more involved

with the distilling, but had to withstand the quarrelling of his sisters, Mary, Isabella (who married Dugald's cousin, Alexander Johnston of Tallant), Margaret and Ann, all of whom disputed the assignation. Walter Graham returned to Lagavulin, but continued to live in Ardenistiel House having taken out 19-year leases in 1852 on the farm, Texa island, and also on the Ardelistry farm for 14 years from 1850.

When Dugald finally took over the reins at Laphroaig he is reputed to have held Walter Graham responsible for not having secured the water rights to the Surnaig burn which already supplied the

Ardenistiel distillery, and which John Morrison had been granted by the Reverend Archibald MacTavish, since the burn ran through his glebe. There is almost certainly more to the story than meets the eye, for Laphroaig's water supply had always been the bog to the north of the public road in any case, and Walter Graham was married to MacTavish's daughter, Elizabeth. The outcome of the quarrel was that Dugald withdrew Laphroaig from sale in the Islay Cellar in Glasgow, which was owned by the Grahams.

After first entering John Cassels in 1852 as the distiller in Ardenistiel, William Hunter took over but gave up the struggle sometime in the 1860s having rarely achieved full production. When Port Ellen was turning over ten washbacks a week, producing 115,000 gallons (552,100 litres) of spirit a year, Ardenistiel managed only 33,000 gallons (149,820 litres) – about half the distillery's potential output. John Ramsay finally decided enough was enough and had the place thrown in with Laphroaig along with the manager's house which was then used by the resident Excise Officer.

Dugald Johnston continued to manage the distillery with Isabella's husband, Alexander Johnston of Tallant, playing an increasing role in the operation before Dugald died in January 1877. At Lagavulin, Walter's brother, John Crawford Graham was in partnership with James Logan Mackie. These two men, together with Colin Hay of Ardbeg were named as Dugald's Trustees, maintaining this position over the course of the next 10 years while Alexander remained in charge of the distillery.

In 1887, the Trustees renounced the lease in favour of John Ramsay and new leases were negotiated and granted to Isabella, her husband Alexander, her sister Mary (by then married to an Alexander Campbell whose exact whereabouts were always in doubt) and their daughter Isabella Campbell. At the same time they 'agreed to pay Mrs Margaret Johnston, or Campbell, sister of the said Dugald Johnston, the sum of £300 Sterling, and to

the family of Mrs Ann Johnston or Brandon, now deceased, also a sister of the said Dugald Johnston, the sum of £100 Sterling . . .'. In effect they had bought out their interests in the distillery. The new leases were for the distillery, with water rights to the Surnaig burn along with peatlands, the farm, Texa island and Torrodale Park, and the buildings which belonged to the Ardenistiel distillery. In all, a quite considerable holding for the time.

Alexander Johnston negotiated new leases in 1904 for the farm and the distillery for a further 15 years, but his wife Isabella died shortly afterwards and his sister Catherine arrived to housekeep for him. She did not conern herself solely with domestic affairs, and must have been a woman far removed from the silk and lace ladies of Edwardian drawing room melo-drama, for when Alexander died in 1907 she promptly took over the running of the distillery. This fact was not lost on Alexander's Trustees, the Edinburgh Writers and Solicitors, Menzies, Bruce-Low and Thomson who were soon to find out how· formidable she was when they informed her that Alexander had made more than one will.

Apparently Alexander had made two or three wills, the last of which benefited his cousin and sister-in-law, Mary and her

*S*andy Johnston (above) took Laphroaig Distillery into the 20th Century before control finally passed into the hands of his sisters and nephew.

daughter Isabella Campbell a great deal more than Catherine thought proper. The second last will was more to Catherine's liking since it favoured herself, her sister Isabella Hunter and their nephew John Johnston Hunter Johnston alone. Naturally, she informed the Trustees that this was the one which would be executed. A letter from Menzies, Bruce-Low and Thomson to Iain Ramsay's factor Peter Reid, dated August 12th 1907 states that 'after providing for a few small legacies under Mr Johnton's will, his sister, Miss Catherine Johnston, is sole beneficiary, so that the whole plant and stock-in-trade at Laphroaig falls to her.' The Trustees then asked Iain Ramsay to renew the leases in the beneficiaries' favour. Whether he was suspicious or just merely curious is not recorded, but he seems to have wanted an explanation as to why the lease should include Isabella. The Trustees came clean, and in the couched language of a law firm which had, strictly speaking, not been playing ball, they replied to Peter Reid on August 26th: AS REGARDS MRS HUNTER *being one of the tenants, along with Miss Johnston and Mr Hunter Johnston, we have to say it will be*

William Stevenson Hunter and his wife Isabella, of Laphroaig.

a disappointment to all three if Mrs Hunter is not one of the tenants. We feel that in putting her name before Mr Ramsay, we did not give a sufficient explanation of her position in relation to the late Mr Johnston's estate; and accordingly we can appreciate the reasonableness of Mr Ramsay entertaining a doubt as to why she should have been brought forward at all. We are now desired to inform you that, by arrangement among Miss Johnston, Mr Hunter Johnston, and Mrs Hunter, the estate of the late Mr Johnston is not to be divided in accordance with the latest in date of his Wills, and that effect is to be given to a great extent to an earlier Will, which was prepared for Mr Johnston by the present writer, under which Will, after providing for certain legacies, including substantial legacies to Miss Johnston, Mrs Hunter, and Mr Hunter Johnston, the residue was to be divided equally among these three. Miss Johnston was good enough to be the first to suggest a departure from the terms of the latest Will; and an Agreement on the subject was signed shortly after Mr Johnston's death. Under this agreement Mrs Hunter will receive a legacy of £1,100, and, over and above that, one third of the ultimate residue. The expectation was that the Laphroaig business would form an important part of the residue.

We may say that our own feeling was that, when we wrote you first proposing the granting of the new Lease, we ought, in justice to Mrs Hunter, to have given you the above explanation; and that we withheld it only in deference to the wishes of Mr Johnston's relatives, who, not unnaturally, were anxious that, if possible, knowledge of their arrangement should be kept to those immediately concerned. They wished to avoid any possibility of the affairs of the late Mr Johnston, and the Wills made by him, being a matter of general discussion. They thought too, that mention of the arrangement might cause a little heartburning on the part of the other relatives of the deceased. For the reasons we have indicated, Mr Ramsay and you will be so good as to receive in confidence the information we have now given.

In view of what we have said, we hope Mr Ramsay will see his way to allow Mrs Hunter to be one of the tenants. The intention has been that she, like her sister and nephew, should leave her share of the estate in the business. Her interest would therefore be a substantial one. It would be for the advantage and convenience of all concerned that she should be a tenant. So far as her circumstances

Laphroaig Distillery staff, 1934. Ian Hunter sits astride the butt, with Iain Ramsay to his left. On the far right the demure secretary, Bessie Williamson, was eventually to become the owner.

are concerned, we think the interest she has in her brother's estate sufficiently warrants her becoming one of the tenants.

Satisfied, but no doubt a little amused by the whole affair, Iain Ramsay did grant a lease to John Johnston Hunter Johnston and his two aunts. Catherine thus followed the MacDougall sisters of Ardbeg and Lucy Ramsay of Port Ellen as one of the first lady distillers in Scotland. But control of Laphroaig had passed into the hands of the Tallant branch of the family and this precipitated much litigation from Alexander's excluded in-laws which forced John to give up the lease and have a new one issued to himself, Catherine, Isabella and her husband William Stevenson Hunter. Their

son, Ian William Hunter was to become the central figure in the development and modernisation of Laphroaig from 1910 onwards. By the time of his father's death in 1919, he had assumed his father's place in the partnership and became sole partner after the deaths of his aunt Catherine in 1926, and his mother the next year. By 1924, he had purchased the distillery, Texa island, and Ardenistiel House from Iain Ramsay, remaining sole proprietor until his death in 1954.

Laphroaig was imported legally into the United States during prohibition as a medicinal spirit thanks to its conveniently ambiguous character. However, these levels of consumption were not high enough to satisfy Ian Hunter, for he had also lost another valuable overseas market due to prohibition, namely, Norway. Having increased capacity from two to four stills in 1923, he continued to sink every last penny into Laphroaig in the belief that things could only get better. The Repeal of

LAPHROAIG DISTILLERY

BY PORT ELLEN, ISLAY, ARGYLL

Owners:
LONG JOHN INTERNATIONAL LTD

123–157 BOTHWELL ST
GLASGOW G2 7AY

Licensees:
D JOHNSTON & CO (LAPHROAIG) LTD

Manager:
MURDO REED

Telephone: 0496 2418

(Visitors should phone in advance. Tours are
usually conducted at 1100 and 1500 hrs.)

Arguably the most famous island malt of all, Laphroaig's situation does not disappoint and gives as much pleasure to the eye as its dram does to the palate. Sheltered in a small cove which is visited by otters and swans, the buildings have undergone little fundamental change for over 100 years. Murdo Reed welcomes all visitors and will often be available to conduct a tour of the entire plant from the 400-tonne barley lofts to the bond directly below his office.

Laphroaig's restful atmosphere is most evident in the floor maltings where Alan Hyslop, the maltman, might be found on a Sunday morning slowly, methodically turning the piece every 3 hours as sunlight, falling through the long row of windows, creates patches of gold on the yellow quilt of barley. The maltings provide a good view of the stillhouse on the other side of the thoroughfare which, like Talisker, contains an odd number of stills – seven in this case.

Laphroaig Distillery's old stillhouse as it was in the 1930s, featuring direct-fired riveted stills (above) and the boiler (left). Installed in 1924, the boiler was replaced in 1955 with a similar type which was floated in from the bay.

Invariably Laphroaig has been said to taste 'medicinal' or 'too much like the sea', but in such a location the sea must naturally influence the character and taste of the maturing whisky. A 'wee sensation' in Murdo's office overlooking the shore helps create an understanding of why Laphroaig tastes '. . . just so!'

Prohibition in 1933 amply rewarded Hunter's foresight.

Around this time a young Glasgow girl, Bessie Williamson, had just graduated and answered an advertisement placed by Hunter for a temporary shorthand typist. Having just taken a business training course, she was hired to help out at the distillery, proving to be so efficient that Hunter offered her the secretary's job on a permanent basis. She could not have suspected then that she would one day rise to the same position which Catherine Johnston had held so tenaciously.

Hunter regained his markets in Scandinavia and began an ambitious promotional tour of the United States before the outbreak of World War II. He first made a call on Thomas Sherriff in Jamaica who had been involved in Bowmore distillery until 1922, and was looking after his sugar plantations and rum distillery. Hunter suffered a slight stroke and was unable to continue the tour so, facing a great loss in potential trade, he cabled Bessie Williamson to join him in Jamaica where he briefed her on his full itinerary. She thus became one of the first promoters of malt whisky on the other side of the Atlantic. Her successful tour was the first of several visits including one to the New York Trade Fair in June 1969 as the representative of the Scotch Whisky Association (SWA).

The importance of Scotch whisky during the war years as a valuable dollar earner was recognised by Ian Hunter but his business drained his health until he was confined to a wheelchair. To safeguard Laphroaig he formed a private company in partnership with his lawyer and accountant, with Bessie Williamson as Company Secretary. She became the driving force at the distillery involving herself in all aspects of management from the malt-house to the bond.

Ian Hunter died at Laphroaig on August 28th 1954 with no heirs. He left not only his entire personal property but also the distillery and the company to Bessie Williamson. She gained a great deal of recognition in the 1950s and 60s and Scotland's 'first lady distiller', which although not strictly true, did no harm to Laphroaig's sales, or to the improved appearance of the distillery.

In the early 1960s the sale of the distillery was negotiated to Long John Distillers Ltd, the subsidiary of the Seager Evans group who added another pair of stills in 1968. Bessie, by then Mrs Wishart Campbell, remained as Managing Director until 1972 before retiring to Ardenistiel House. In 1970, control passed to a newly-formed company, Long John International who were themselves taken over in 1975 by Whitbread & Co Ltd, the brewers.

Further expansion took place in 1974 when another still was added, and just recently the entire stillhouse was remodelled during the distilling season without a single day's production being lost, something of which the manager, Murdo Reed, can be justifiably proud. In the space of a century, Laphroaig has gone from being a family concern to an important part of the portfolio of a major British company, without its product having changed significantly. Laphroaig's success and current good health in an industry suffering its worst recession in living memory is a testament to the enduring high quality of the spirit made in 'the hollow by the bay.'

Bessie Williamson (above) checking the spirit in the old Laphroaig stillhouse. Port Ellen Distillery and Maltings (above right).

PORT ELLEN

Any visitor to Islay about to disembark at Port Askaig will be struck by the bleak hills and deep glens behind McArthur's Head at the mouth of the Sound of Islay. This solitary region holds the attention of the unfamiliar traveller from many miles distant until the ferry is ready to berth. It displays many of those features for which much of Islay is famous – dark, sombre corries amongst high rolling hills commanding views to Kintyre with a total lack of human habitation. The development of the distillery at Port Ellen owes much to the determination of a young midland Scot who was forced to make landfall near McArthur's Head in 1833 and then make his way overland to Port Ellen.

John Ramsay was then only 18 and the nephew of the Procurator Fiscal of Clackmannan, Ebenezer Ramsay, who was in charge of the extensive distilling interests which the family fostered around Alloa. John's cousin John Morrison had been placed in charge of the distillery which had been developed from a malt mill

erected by Alexander Kerr MacKay in 1825 with Walter Frederick Campbell's approval and converted during the next few years into a distillery.

These formative years show how complicated the lease arrangements were in those days. MacKay held the ground lease for the distillery, while the lease for the buildings was held by Major James Adair of Dumfries and Glasgow, who in turn sub-let to John Morrison and his associates, George MacLennan and Patrick Thomson. Despite this curious situation, it was MacKay who appears to have held the reins, for when £300 was granted by Adair in 1831 for 'improvements and additions to Port Ellen Distillery and its utensils' it was MacKay who had requested the aid on Morrison's behalf. Only when MacKay died in 1833 did Adair finally gain complete control by purchasing the ground lease from MacKay's assignee Michael Rowand Ronald.

Things did not go well at Port Ellen under John Morrison's management and Ebenezer despatched his son Eben to report back, but receiving no word from him he started John Ramsay on his precarious journey to finally sort things out. His uninspiring landing near Gleann Choiredail left him with a 12-mile (19-km) hike guided only by a compass and a wealth of good common sense. Unknown to him, Eben was at that moment sailing for the mainland on the very winds which had forced John onto the opposite side of the island.

Completing the last few miles on a pony lent to him by the MacDougalls of Arivochallum, he arrived at Port Ellen to learn from John Morrison that Eben was to report to his father that the distillery was unworkable. This, John was soon to realise, was not the case and he informed his uncle that the operation had a future in the right hands. With the timely arrival of his elder brother, Thomas, from New Brunswick, a new partnership was formed whereby Morrison was to enter the Glasgow office to take charge of sales, Thomas was to manage grain supplies and John, after training as a distiller under Morrison's brother James in Alloa, was to run the distillery at an annual salary of £150. Eben meanwhile, clearly had had enough of the whole affair, and disappeared to New Orleans where his uncle James was a merchant.

The arrangement, however, was unsuccessful from the start. Thomas Ramsay soon realised that John Morrison was an impossible partner and quit, following Eben across the Atlantic where it is believed he lost his life in the Mexican War of 1836-7. Although barely in his twenties, John Ramsay was already creating very favourable impressions with the many businessmen he dealt with in Glasgow and Islay and Adair, who had lost a leg at Waterloo in the year of John's birth, allowed him free rein to establish his business. Within a year Ebenezer's second son, and John Ramsay's cousin, also called Thomas, joined the partnership to the exclusion of the unfortunate John Morrison who was eventually to take over in 1837 from his cousin James Stein in Ardenistiel distillery by Laphroaig.

Under Ramsay's management the distillery gradually expanded with a second duty free warehouse being added in 1839 due to his 'present increased business'. He was, however, only a tenant and after Adair died in 1840 the leases became vacant and the distillery was put up for sale. John Ramsay badly needed the leases if he was to consolidate his business interests in Port Ellen, but legally the distillery and the leases were up for auction to the highest bidder. Alexander Craig of Wadeston Mills, Glasgow entered the highest bid of £1,950 but was unable to secure the sale because the laird, Walter Frederick Campbell, had been so impressed with Ramsay's ability that he exercised his right of preemption at the expiry of the leases and matched Craig's bid, thus assuring Ramsay the distillery, and a new lease. Once Ramsay had repaid the laird he took out leases on two neighbouring farms at Cornabus and Kilnaughton, finally settling in Port Ellen as farmer and distiller.

By 1842, his inventory showed 7,399 gallons (33,590 litres) of whisky in bond worth £1,479 16s out of a whole stock in hand including barley, bere, peats, coals, and feints amounting to £4,193 19s 8d.

Much of his early business success was due to trade with North America by direct export from Port Ellen. As the distiller's spokesman, he actively sought the lifting of restrictions in 1848 which allowed spirits to be exported in casks exceeding 80 gallons capacity and the right to store whisky in bond duty free for export. The Port Ellen warehouses are not only some of the earliest constructed for this purpose, but are reputed to be amongst the best.

By this time his sister Margaret had joined him at Cornabus farm and married James Stein who had been managing Ardenistiel distillery with his brother Andrew. Stein became Ramsay's factor and distillery manager, effectively freeing him to attend to his affairs in Glasgow where he imported Sherry and Madeira wine, and coincidentally had a house in Madeira Court. Together they were to refine the spirit safe which had been invented in the early 1820s by Septimus Fox and adopted by the Excise after the Act of 1823.

Just as Walter Frederick Campbell's

estate was about to collapse, so John Ramsay's grew, largely due to fortuitous inheritance and astute management on his part. He was gifted with a great feel for the land and became one of Islay's leading agriculturalists voicing his opinions on farming matters as a regular contributor to the *Glasgow Herald*. Campbell sought and doubtless took heed of Ramsay's advice in a last ditch effort to sort out the affairs of his badly managed estate, but as Joseph Mitchell, one of Thomas Telford's roving engineers, observed around this time, 'unfortunately Mr Campbell was no man of business.' In fairness, the laird had become the victim of circumstances far outwith his control, and it was too late for John Ramsay's good judgement and sound business advice to save him.

Campbell's estate passed to the English merchant James Morrison who agreed the sale of Kildalton to Ramsay in 1855 for £70,765 thus becoming landlord to the Johnstons of Laphroaig, the Grahams of Lagavulin and the MacDougalls of Ardbeg. Ramsay's other interests were just as diverse having started the weekly steamer service between Islay and Glasgow and instigated the construction of new roads throughout Kildalton. His business in Port Ellen no longer required his full-time attention which he now gave to politics and public service. When it became apparent to him that there was insufficient food grown on the island to feed all of his tenants, he encouraged the more able amongst them to emigrate to Canada. The manner in which this was carried out says a great deal for his humanity and common sense and many of the Islay families crossed the Atlantic at his expense to build new futures in Canada's eastern provinces. He visited them in 1870 and was pleased to see them well established, as his granddaughter-in-law Freda Ramsay recorded 100 years later: *A*LL *THROUGH HURONIA AND THE townships northeast of Lake Simcoe it is possible to see fine farms, with the delightful houses which succeeded the log cabins, still occupied by descendants of the men and women with whom John Ramsay talked during his visit. Many of the younger generations have spread across the length and breadth of North America and the prosperity and happiness they have created for themselves is the finest memorial John Ramsay could have wished.*

The Glasgow end of the business had been managed by John Morrison, followed by James Richardson and then W P Lowrie, who left in 1869 to start up on his own, successfully blending and bottling Scotch in bond. Although he was later erroneously credited for having initiated these practices in Scotland, he did introduce some innovation into the production and marketing of Scotch which remain with us today. He was the first to pre-treat casks when a scarcity of sherry butts for fillings occurred in the late 19th Century and he installed a large bottling plant at his works in Washington Street, Glasgow, which effectively made his operation self-contained.

Three years before his death in 1892 John Ramsay granted a lease to his second wife Lucy for the land on the seaward side of the distillery, where she built four villas – one for herself should her daughter ever marry, and the others for distillery and Excise workers. Her involvement in the distillery deepened when Ramsay died at Kildalton House on January 24th 1892, aged 77 and the day-to-day running of the business passed to her. In September, a special meeting was convened to determine 'payments to Mrs Ramsay for spirits at Port Ellen, sold during John Ramsay's lifetime but not delivered' which stood at 160,287 gallons (727,700 litres) at the end of June, 1892. The valuators were A W Robertson of Robertson and Baxter, the Glasgow whisky brokers, and W P Lowrie and between them they fixed the prices of the peats, feints, malt and coals taken over by Mrs Ramsay as follows:

1,200 carts of peats at 2s a cart.
359 gallons feints at 1s per proof gallon.
400 bushels of Malt at 25s a quarter.
25 tons coals at 10s a ton.

At the same time it was decided that John Ramsay's grand-nephew and manager, J R Stein, would leave the firm no later than

September 30th with a final paycheck for £16 13s 4d.

An eminently practical woman, who had never favoured Stein, Lucy Ramsay then took over with a Mr Osborne as manager until her death in 1905. Her son Iain Ramsay, aged 27, took back the distillery while his mother's capital in the plant was inherited by his sister, Miss Lucy. From this point on Iain Ramsay was to struggle as best he could to keep the distillery business on a sound footing, and he was forced to find a business partner in 1912, when his sister decided to lift her capital from the business to buy an estate on the mainland. At that time, he was employing Malcolm MacIntyre of Train and MacIntyre Ltd, as a trainee distiller and agreed to take him in just as the Great War loomed.

Ramsay and MacIntyre both joined up but only Ramsay survived, returning as an invalided Captain to find his business in want of capital, and his markets rapidly receding due to the effects of war and the introduction of prohibition in America. He was in bad health, his stored household effects had all been destroyed in a Zeppelin raid and he was forced to sell off his assets and parts of his estate in order to maintain the remainder.

W P Lowrie had fared better and his firm was then owned by James Buchanan & Co Ltd since Lowrie's retirement in 1906. For years Lowrie had acted as Buchanan's main supplier and no doubt his intimate knowledge of Port Ellen distillery may have moved Buchanan to acquire the distillery and its assets in partnership with John Dewar & Sons Ltd in 1920 as the Port Ellen Distillery Co Ltd.

After the final merging of Buchanan-Dewar with the DCL in 1925, Port Ellen was absorbed into the group until the company was voluntarily liquidated 2 years later as part of the DCL's rationalisation programme – due largely to the effects of the Depression. The assets were then acquired by John Dewar & Son Ltd and W P Lowrie & Co Ltd before being finally transferred to SMD in 1930. At this time the DCL and its subsidiaries were taking over the largest and finest stocks of maturing whisky anywhere in Scotland and although Port Ellen was officially closed in 1930 due to the depression and general economic climate, there can be no doubt that the distillery possessed an extensive stock in bond. At that time there was enough whisky warehoused in Port Ellen to last 40 years, and the more cynical observers today remind you that it was fully 37 years before the distillery came on stream again.

In order 'to meet the needs of its blending companies, The Distillers Company Limited decided to bring Port Ellen back into production' in the mid-1960s. The industry in general was expanding around this time with Charles Mackinlay's Jura distillery once more in production and a great deal of development being carried out in the Highlands, enabling the malt sector to double its output during the decade.

Port Ellen became an extremely efficient distillery after rebuilding which was completed in April 1967. Fortunately some of the original buildings were retained but the character of the shoreside site was irretrievably changed in 1973 when the maltings were erected. Capable of producing 400 tonnes of malted barley each week, the maltings initially supplied all three SMD distilleries on Islay making their floor maltings redundant. But the curious spectacle of loads of malt being trucked the short distance around the block to Port Ellen distillery ceased in May 1983 when it was one of the 11 SMD distilleries closed by the DCL in their efforts to cut back production.

Why did such an efficient distillery have to close? The DCL stated: *I*TS CLOSURE WAS *part of the measures taken by Scottish Malt Distillers to reduce output in order to bring the level of maturing stock into line with the anticipated level of future sales.*

There is no doubt that the DCL had to make a very difficult decision in both human and economic terms, but these are naturally exacerbated in an island

*P*ort Ellen Distillery workers (above) at the turn of the century with the formidable Mr Osborne in the centre. Malcolm MacIntyre (right), who followed Lucy Ramsay (far right), as a partner with Lucy's son, Iain.

community and the decision to close Port Ellen does not appear to have been taken with these factors in mind. Transport costs from the islands are such that higher savings can be made by the closure of a distillery like Port Ellen. Having decided on an island closure, Port Ellen may well have been chosen because of the far greater reputation of Caol Ila, Lagavulin and Talisker within the blending trade, notwithstanding the popularity of the last two as single malts.

Although renowned as a company insensitive to criticism, the DCL must have taken note of the unfavourable press which Highland Distilleries received in March 1982 when Bunnahabhain was closed and almost the entire community around the distillery was made redundant. On all counts, Port Ellen was the most likely candidate. In a town with an unemployment rate of 20%, the effects were spelt out in the local paper, the *Ileach* in terms which the board of the DCL may not have fully appreciated at the time: *T*HERE WILL BE *less draff so the farmers will suffer as will Willie Currie's haulage business. Mundell's transport will lose half a day's work involved in taking malt from maltings to distillery, and two loads of whisky to the ferry per week. The loss of 20 distillery pay packets will be felt in the shops, pubs and service industries of Port Ellen.*

PORT ELLEN DISTILLERY AND MALTINGS

PORT ELLEN, ISLAY, ARGYLL

Owners:
SCOTTISH MALT DISTILLERS
TRINITY RD ELGIN
MORAYSHIRE IV30 1UF

Licensees:
LOW ROBERTSON & CO LTD
10 LINKS PLACE
LEITH, EDINBURGH EH6 7HA

Maltings Manager:
E CATTANACH
Telephone: 0496 2315

(Visits should be arranged through the
SMD at the Elgin office.
Telephone: 0343 7891)

The last thing you see when you leave Port Ellen to cross the Laggan Bog to Bowmore is the huge 30-metre high maltings plant dwarfing the silent distillery below it on the shore road. Impressive it may be, but when the January gales of 1984 lashed the coast, they ran over the distillery and gave the high-sided facade an expensive battering.

A more incongruous structure is hard to imagine in such a place and it comes as a surprise to hear that it is only working at half capacity supplying Lagavulin and Caol Ila – could other Islay distilleries not benefit from such a convenient source of malted barley? DCL policy prevents them from being supplied, which in the present economic climate seems a little short-sighted. At least one other distillery manager on Islay felt that the plant could supply another two distilleries with what is generally regarded as the finest quality malt available.

That said, Ernie Cattanach, the ebullient manager of the Maltings is only too pleased to show off the internal workings of the cavernous structure. If Barnard were to experience this amount of hardware today his reaction would be one of complete disbelief – only a good look round brings home the sheer scale of the operation. Meanwhile, the distillery sleeps, a sad memorial to John Ramsay who, operating from here, pioneered the export of malt whisky to the Americas, creating markets on which the trade now greatly depends. It is unfitting that his foresight and perseverance are no longer manifested in his most conspicuous achievement in Port Ellen.

Two roads cross the immense Laggan Bog between Port Ellen and Bowmore – a high road (B8016) which emerges near Bridgend, and the more recent low road (A846) which runs straight over the flatter expanse of moor for some 10 miles (16 km). The former route has changed little since Barnard's visit when he took over 4 hours to reach Bridgend, describing it as 'such a dismal and lonely road.' Halfway across the bog Laphroaig's peat is hand-cut for the next

Port Ellen Disillery in 1904 (below) showing Lucy Ramsay's villas on the right.

THE DISTILLERY, PORT ELLEN, ISLAY

distilling season by Alec Johnston and Micky Heads.

Some 800 to 1,000 tonnes are lifted between April and June each year in characteristic long, square-section sods and, once dry, stacked crosswise in tiers of two upon two, seven layers high until ready to take down to Laphroaig. But it is not the work it was. 'There's no piece work now, no weekend work at all. Five years ago I could make £150 a week at this working my own hours – now everything is set,' Alec recalls.

The bog extends to the very edge of Bowmore and surveys suggest that it is at least 30 feet (9 metres) deep at some points – so long as barley is malted on Islay, there will be peat enough to dry it.

BOWMORE

The establishment of a distillery in Bowmore at the foot of Hill Street was a natural development in the early industrial evolution of the village. With hindsight it is too easy to conclude that the modest operation, which probably started just as the village began to take shape in 1768, was of little immediate benefit to the community but after two centuries of almost continuous production the vision of the Campbells has been realised.

The early history of the distillery can only be surmised, but an understanding of the way in which many of the leases were contracted in those days leads one to believe that David Simson was distilling much earlier than 1779, as has been thought. When Daniel Campbell the Younger decided to build Bowmore and move the island's social and economic centre from Killarow (now Bridgend) he granted many new leases for the village through his chief feuar, Hugh Mackay. Most of these were settled with a handshake, and remained so until the

The village of Bowmore in 1772 shortly after it was established by Daniel Campbell the 'Younger', showing the famous round church at far left and the beginnings of the distillery to the right of the village.

growing liabilities of tenant and laird alike made a more formal contract necessary. In Bowmore's case these written leases first appear in 1766, when Campbell had a feu charter drawn up between himself and Simson for a 'rood of land and square acres of Moss.' These were soon supplemented with 'a piece of ground in Hill Street and Shore Street.'

In 1776, one year before he died, Daniel Campbell granted rights to Simson 'to build and erect dwelling houses and other houses and to quarry, win and load stones for these purposes, and to cut, win and load turf from the moss.'

So what happened during the 10 years between these agreements? Simson created the mould from which all the other commercially successful island distillers were drawn. He was a merchant and farmer alike and had been distilling at Killarow for some time until he quit to move to Bowmore around 1766. Donald MacEachern then took over at Killarow, and local knowledge suggests that Simson started building his new distillery almost immediately.

He clearly had a great deal of energy since he also acted as postmaster between 1767 and 1775, and claimed to be in the same position in 1790. He had also been responsible for the running of the Islay packet from Tarbert, Argyll to Port Askaig, although he was none too successful in that venture. He was far better as a distiller, and by securing a feu for Bowmore Distillery it meant that he actually owned the ground as opposed to leased it. Built during a time of common grain shortages the output of Bowmore would have reflected this influence – men like Simson did well to maintain their small operations, particularly in the face of the illicit distillers. He felt strongly about this and at the biannual meeting of the Stent Committee in March 1801, he was one of the signatories to the pledge that: *T*HIS

meeting resolve collectively & individually to use their utmost exertions for preventing any of the grain of the Island being destroy'd by illegal Distillers, and for that purpose pledge themselves to inform agt any person or persons that they may know or hear to be concerned in this illegal and destructive Traffick.

Simson is believed to have extended his distilling activities to Jura for a while but this was shortlived. The distance from Bowmore and the access during the winter months created too many problems and he concentrated his business on Islay. Eventually he relinquished control to Hector Simson who had a new water course built in 1825 which the estate financed. An entry in the Rent Roll reads: *I*NTEREST TO *be charged to H Simson on £65, the sum expended in making Distillery Canal at 7½ per cent.*

The laird further encouraged distilling by extending credit in the form of barley to Simson who repaid this when the whisky was sold in Glasgow. In 1827, barley worth £756 was advanced in this manner to Simson and rent was frequently paid to the laird by the farmers in the form of grain.

In 1837 the distillery changed hands to William and James Mutter, Glasgow merchants of German extraction, who began a programme of expansion and renovation. James Mutter was a philanthropist and a progressive farmer in the same mould as the Campbells and John Ramsay. Besides leasing three farms on Islay, he found time to be the Ottoman, Portuguese and Brazilian Vice-Consul in Glasgow.

Under the Mutters new kilns, warehouses and tun rooms were built and the stillhouse was enlarged featuring a still with forked head! The amount of water reaching the distillery was increased by rerouting the lade from the River Laggan. A local tailor is credited with overcoming the problems of a lack of fall over the new course by observing the movement of drops of water along a length of waxed thread. The resulting course of the lade is thus some 9 miles (14½ km) although the source is only half this distance from the distillery.

A 145-ton iron steamship, not surprisingly named the SS *James Mutter*, was commissioned to ply between Islay and Glasgow where the Mutters had warehouse facilities beneath the arches of Central Station. Bowmore became a renowned single malt sold in various export markets and in England was purveyed successfully by a number of travelling salesmen. When Barnard looked around Bowmore, the distillery was producing 200,000 gallons of spirit (908,000 litres) per annum. Only Ardbeg could boast a greater volume on the island.

The sons of the Mutter brothers ran the distillery until 1892, when it was sold to a consortium from London in a sale which was disputed. The outcome was The Bowmore Distillery Company which controlled the operation through the bleak war years until 1925 when J B Sherriff & Co bought it for £20,000. This company had originally been formed in 1895 to acquire the Lochhead distillery in Campbeltown

*T*he cutting of peat for home and distillery
is a centuries-old activity on Islay. Women
used to help in the removal of hundreds of
tonnes each year (top). Nowadays, only two
cutters, Micky Heads and Alec Johnston
(right) meet Laphroaig's total needs
compared with a workforce of at least 12 at
Ardbeg around 1912 (above). Some things
never change though – Bowmore's copper
mashtun is a timeless feature.

and the Lochindaal distillery at Port Charlotte, along with sugar plantations and a rum distillery in Jamaica. In 1920 Sherriffs were forced into liquidation and both distilleries were acquired by Benmore Distilleries who maintained them until being absorbed by the DCL in 1929. Lochhead closed for good in 1928 followed by Lochindaal just after the DCL takeover. It was then dismantled, although the bonds still exist and are used by Caol Ila distillery.

After the liquidation, J B Sherriff & Co Ltd was sold to J P O' Brien Ltd exactly one day after that firm itself had passed a resolution for voluntary liquidation. They had just purchased Bulloch, Lade, owners of Caol Ila, one month before and appear to have been in no position to hold onto assets so both J B Sherriff and Bulloch, Lade found ready buyers at knockdown prices. The name and goodwill of Sherriffs were purchased for £100 in shares by a Skyeman, Duncan MacLeod of Skeabost who had also been a director of Bulloch, Lade and the Highland Bonding Company. A new company bearing the name of J B Sherriff was then formed in December 1924, purchased Bowmore the following year, and ran it under Sherriff's Bowmore Distillery Ltd. The resurrection lasted until 1950 when William Grigor & Son Ltd of Inverness, who had been responsible for the rebuilding of the Glen Albyn Distillery in 1884, took them over.

The intervening war years had seen the distillery unproductive, like many others, due to the Government's prohibition on distilling. Bowmore was requisitioned by the Air Ministry to serve as the operations centre for Coastal Command giving anti-submarine assistance to Atlantic convoys. Bowmore was not alone amongst the island distilleries in this – Tobermory was put to use by the Navy during World War II.

Stanley P Morrison Ltd, the Glasgow whisky brokers, moved into distilling in 1963 by purchasing the company at a time when many disused distilleries, like Jura, were being recommissioned. The expansion of trade in the 1960s resulted in malt whisky output rising from 65 million litres of pure alcohol (LPA) to 124 million LPA

in 1968. In this atmosphere Morrisons instigated a period of modernisation and expansion.

When Morrisons made their purchase, it was the first in a series of steps taking them to the forefront of the small independents in the whisky industry. The Roseburn Bonding Company was soon added to extend storage and create valuable blending facilities in Glasgow and this was followed with the Tannochside Bonding Company in 1965, where new warehousing was built to hold 5 million gallons (22.7 million litres) of spirit. Their distilling interests were further increased in 1970 when they bought Glengarioch Distillery near Old Meldrum in Aberdeenshire from SMD, and more recently the Auchentoshan Distillery near Glasgow producing a triple-distilled malt which has risen to 6th place in the export league of bottled malts.

All island distilleries suffer from high overheads largely due to transportation costs to and from the mainland – in Bowmore's case these costs amounted to £100,000 per annum. In attempting to overcome these, Morrisons tried to find a means to offset them against savings from reduced fuel consumption. Fuel bills within the industry in 1970 accounted for some 9% of production costs, rising to 16% by 1980. They had already had some success at Glengarioch by employing a waste heat recovery system which was used to create perfect growing environments for tomatoes in glasshouses built next to the distillery. With a ready market for the produce in the Aberdeenshire area the project gradually expanded to 145 tonnes per annum and has proved profitable while savings amounting to over £90,000 per annum have been possible.

With the experience gained from the Glengarioch project, the company sought a similar solution for Bowmore. A glasshouse project was rejected due to the lack of surrounding suitable ground and the small market amongst Islay's 4,000 residents. The energy consultants Derick Sampson & Partners of Glasgow designed a waste heat recovery system which was to reduce the

fuel costs by 50% with a payback on capital investment in less than 3 years.

The new system operated on the principle that steam could be created at low temperatures in the presence of a vacuum located in the vapour head on the still condensers. Sufficient quantities of 'flash' steam were thus generated not only to heat the stills, but also the coppers. Another benefit was the conversion of the kiln to indirect heating by means of a water/air heat exchanger drawing hot water from the condensers surplus to process requirements, eliminating completely the heavy fuel oil which was then in use as the primary heat source.

The capital outlay required was £274,000, but annual fuel savings were estimated to run to £104,500. These were very attractive figures for Morrisons' board to contemplate but there was one major drawback – the effect which the change in

The characteristic outline of Bowmore (above) still dominates the town's skyline, just as it continues to dominate the local economy. Pioneering attitudes to public relations at Stanley P Morrison Ltd have ensured that the distillery reception centre is kept busy during the tourist season.

the way the stills were heated would have on the whisky. Despite this reservation the plan was approved in early 1983, with installation taking place during the annual shutdown in the summer.

The industry is watching the outcome of the Bowmore development with interest but is unlikely to follow its example until the matured stocks of 1983 Bowmore emerge from the bond. The real success of the project will depend on the undiminished quality and character of the whisky, only then is Morrisons' example likely to be followed. Time will tell.

The Alystra moored in the calm of an island evening (far left). Bowmore's vaults are sunk deep into the ground close to the sea (top). Moisture seeps into the earthen floors creating an atmosphere ". . . perfect for making whisky. . .", as manager Jim McEwan expounds. John Ramsay's 21-year-old vatted malt, 'Dunaid', (above) was named after the promontory on the Oa's southern coast (left).

BOWMORE DISTILLERY
BOWMORE, ISLAY, ARGYLL

Owners:
STANLEY P MORRISON LTD
SPRINGBURN BOND, CARLISLE STREET, GLASGOW

Licensees:
MORRISON'S BOWMORE DISTILLERY LTD

Manager:
JAMES MCEWAN
Telephone: 049681 441/2/3

(There are conducted tours at 1030 and
1430 hrs. Mon-Fri.)

A 19th-Century advertisement for Bowmore (above), intended for the Canadian market.

Literally built into the harbour wall, the distillery appears at times to almost merge with the waters of Loch Indaal. In such an inviting situation, Bowmore not surprisingly offers the visitor the most comprehensive facilities of any island distillery with a modern, capacious and well appointed reception centre, which also serves as a local community hall. The manager, Jim McEwan, has an intimate knowledge of Bowmore. Born in the town, he trained as a cooper here before spending 8 years in Glasgow as a blender with Morrisons. As a cooper he could not have had a more experienced master than David Bell. Now appoaching 90, he retired in 1970 having been Scotland's number 1 or most senior cooper for 8 years – the craftsmen are numbered according to their seniority and when David started in 1914 he was 300th in line. As an apprentice he then earned 10s a week, rising to £3-£4 on piece work in Glasgow before World War II. When he retired he was building three butts a day and taking home £60-£70 a week. Dressed in worn tweeds, topped off with a flat cap and *Gardener's Hints* sticking from his top pocket, David frequently drops into the distillery to 'rescue' any odd items that 'are surely going to be thrown out anyway.' At times like this, the relationship between these two old friends is something to see.

Jim's go-ahead attitude befits Bowmore, which is recognised as one of the busiest and most popular in Scotland. The existence of new techniques within the framework of such an old distillery makes it one of the most rewarding of all to visit. The bonds, however, remain unchanged, no modern influences can alter the way in which whisky matures. To the rear of the stillhouse, through a cramped alley, the old vaults lie, sunk deep into the sloping ground. Inside, row upon row of butts and hogsheads are racked in the traditional manner by 'dunnage'. One of the sherry butts stands out from the body of casks. Beautifully crafted it was made by Tommy Williamson, recently retired from Robertson & Baxter as manager of their Clyde Cooperage. He took particular care with this one – it was presented to Her Majesty the Queen during her visit to Islay in 1981 and will remain there until ready for

Davy Bell gives a little assistance while Ian Gillies, the present Bowmore cooper, wields a 'devil'.

the Queen's Cellar. Islay malt is no stranger to the Royal Household – on Christmas Eve 1841 this letter was sent from Windsor Castle to the laird.

My Dear Islay,

Will you undertake a commission and oblige me by ordering or procuring for me (or rather for the Queen's Cellar) a cask of your best Islay Mountain Dew? I am not very particular as to the exact quantity contained by the cask nor as to the price, but I want the very best that can be had, for which reason I prefer troubling you to ordering it blindfold from any merchant . . . We are all in great turmoil here preparing for the reception of all sorts of Royalties and Principalities at the Christening of the P of Wales. I expect no peace or quiet till it is over!

> *Believe me my dear chief.*
> *yrs very faithfully*
> *Ch A Murray*

The 'Dew' was obviously a great favourite at the Palace – just over 2 years later Murray repeated the request for another 120 gallons (545 litres), beseeching Campbell to put the distiller 'on his mettle to give us his best brew . . .' and reminding him to pay particular attention to the 'Excise Drawback, for the Queen's spirits pay no duty . . .'! It was in fact John Ramsay who supplied the Palace, with a special 21-year-old vatted malt which he called 'Dunaid'.

He named this extraordinary whisky after Dunaid, a small promontory on the southern side of the Oa which he considered to be Islay's most interesting antiquity. The Oa abounds with names of Norse origin and Ramsay felt that Dunaid was the most likely site of any island court which the Norsemen might have held, since it so closely resembled Thingvalla in Iceland which was used for that purpose. The small neck of land joining Dunaid to the mainland would have been easily defended by a small number of armed men, making a surprise attack impossible. Later, the Lords of the Isles employed the same strategy at Finlaggan by holding court on the islet in the Loch.

The whisky itself was an interesting marriage of Port Ellen (which could only have been 16 years old at the most) and 21-year-old Upper Cragabus, which Ramsay claimed was the finest whisky ever produced on Islay. Unfortunately a great deal of the production from this area was illicit and there is a good chance that some of this may have found its way into the Royal cask. When the MacCuaigs were producing legal whisky at Cragabus it is reputed that the profits from the exports to Ireland went into establishing the shorefront White Hart Hotel in Port Ellen – so much for being built on foundations of sand!

Copper abounds inside Bowmore, from the stills to the coppers themselves. In many distilleries clinical stainless steel has taken over almost entirely in the mash and tun rooms, but not here – the gleaming, burnished, at times almost iridescent metal, is everywhere, increasing the voyeur's pleasure. At the bar in the reception centre, where all sorts of promotional items can be had, Jim pours a generous dram of Bowmore, 12 years old and straight from the cask. The aroma of burnt peat and chocolate rise from the glass, no other terms can describe it adequately. It is a good dram, especially when savoured along with the view under a blue sky over Loch Indaal to Bruichladdich, one of the next stops beyond Bridgend at the head of the loch.

BRUICHLADDICH, BUNNAHABHAIN AND CAOL ILA

All three distilleries share their names with small villages which were built up around them, creating their own communities dependent on them for employment. In the case of Caol Ila and Bunnahabhain in particular, it is likely that without the distilleries there would have been no sustained human interference in the area at all. There, the workers' houses were constructed at the same time as the distilleries, and even today are almost all owned by the companies operating the plants.

Caol Ila lies just north of Port Askaig on the Sound of Islay at the end of a tortuous cul-de-sac over-looking the Paps of Jura. It was built in 1846 by a Glasgow businessman with extensive distilling interests. Hector Henderson had been a partner in the Campbeltown Distillery in 1837, and having just withdrawn from the Littlemill Distillery near Bowling, Dunbartonshire, was looking for a suitable site for a new distillery and, for reasons known only to himself, he chose the remote Islay location. It is a surprising site for a distillery, and when Alfred Barnard made his way to Caol Ila in 1886 the approach had not changed in 40 years: *WE SOON CAME IN SIGHT OF the distillery lying directly beneath us, and we wonder for a moment how we are to get down to it. Our driver, however, knew the road well, for often had he been here before, and turning sharp to the right, we commenced the descent through the little hamlet of houses. But the way is so steep, and our nerves none of the best, that we insist upon doing the remainder of the descent on foot, much to the disgust of the driver, who muttered strange words in Gaelic. His remarks, however, are lost upon us, that language not having formed part of our education. As we descended the hill, we paused now and then to gaze upon the far stretching view before us, and to rest.*

Presently we found ourselves at the object of our search, and within a few yards of the sea. Caol Ila Distillery stands in the wildest and most picturesque locality we have seen. It is situated on the Sound of Islay on the very verge of the sea, in a deep recess of the mountain mostly cut out of the solid rock. The coast hereabouts is wild and broken, and detached pieces of rock lie here and there of such size that they form small islands.

To the Victorian reader this description was very much in the style of the times, but to be fair to Barnard the route is largely unchanged today, and is still impressive.

Henderson may have been attracted by the exceptionally pure source of water from Torrabolls Loch, but it is more likely that the laird, his estate on the verge of bankruptcy, recognised a perfectly good opportunity to extend Islay's distilling industry which had become a major source of employment on the island. After the worst depression of the 19th Century, during which 61 distilleries closed between 1835 and 1844, confidence in the malt sector in the face of increasing competition from the Lowland distillers was very low. However, the Islay malts were still highly

The Pibroch *ties up alongside the* Polarlight *to unload coal at Port Askaig with the Paps of Jura beyond. Both vessels are owned by Glenlight Shipping.*

*C*aol Ila's bold modern facade has become a
familiar sight on the Sound of Islay since it
was completed in 1974 (right). The sheer size
of the stills is hard to comprehend when seen
against the backdrop of the Paps of Jura (above).
Even so, the possibility of stills collapsing
due to a vacuum forming when they are emptied still
exists, as John Ramsay was aware in 1840
". . .the air cock must however be turned. . .
Carelessness in this particular has often destroyed
the still by the pressure of air collapsing the still."
There is little chance of this happening to
any of the six copper stills in Caol Ila,
since nowadays the stillhouse has a
centralised control panel and is
fully automated.

regarded as flavoursome drams in comparison to the bland Lowland whisky. Walter Frederick Campbell, for his part, had helped establish or legalise around a dozen distilleries during his lairdship of Islay, though not all of them had lasted as long as he would have liked. These included Daill, Newton, Tallant, Lossit and Mulindry which were all large farm distilleries with illicit beginnings.

In 1847 Henderson sunk his money not only into Caol Ila but also Camlachie Distillery, Glasgow, and installed larger pot stills 2 years later. In 1849 the ground lease for Caol Ila was granted to an unknown William Campbell, who may possibly have been a financier in the same style as many of the Kildalton operators and by 1850, Henderson had entered a partnership to acquire Lochindaal Distillery at Port Charlotte. All the signs point to Henderson extending his business too quickly, and by 1852 Henderson Lamont & Co was forced to stop trading altogether.

The industry at this time was having to contend with an influential temperance movement with widespread support and a Government which sought to equalise the duty on spirits throughout the United Kingdom. This meant that Scottish producers had to withstand rises in duty which brought them up to the higher levels at which the English had operated for many years. Some distillers could not absorb these increases and, coupled with a general decline in whisky consumption in Scotland, they folded. Between 1850 and 1857, there were over 30 closures in Scotland, most of which occurred in rural areas where they had used locally-grown barley, thus benefiting from the malt drawback until Gladstone abolished it in 1855.

Collapses of this nature had a restricting effect on the industry in general, but the sequestration of Henderson Lamont & Co did at least allow Norman Buchanan of the Jura Distillery to take over Caol Ila. Buchanan was barely set up in Jura when Henderson went under, so he jumped at the chance to enter an almost new plant just across the Sound. When his business was sequestered in 1863 he was probably wishing he had concentrated on Jura – once more Caol Ila was ownerless.

In the meantime developments had taken place at Henderson's other distillery at Camlachie. It had been purchased by Bulloch & Co, who were trading 3 years later as Bulloch, Lade & Co and were to remain in control for the next 61 years. When Caol Ila came on the market in 1863 they acquired it, realising an excellent opportunity to buy a malt which had a good reputation in the growing blending trade. Bulloch, Lade were even then a large company dealing mainly with the trade as blenders and commission agents, with outlets at home and abroad. Their success enabled them to build the Benmore Distillery in Campbeltown in 1868 and carry out major improvements at Caol Ila in 1879. At the time of Barnard's visit, it was one of the most modern in existence, producing 147,000 gallons (667,000 litres) per annum.

The 1880s represented a decade of expansion for the malt producers. Blended whiskies were then so well accepted that they sold in almost every country in the world – some of them with brand names still in existence today. Many of the heavy island malts were used by blenders to mask the bland Lowland whiskies in their products and thus give them more character. This growing demand for malt led to the distillers expanding out of their low capital investment operations and building units capable of higher outputs. Other Lowland distillers like Bulloch, Lade looked for suitable opportunities to expand their business. This led to the construction of both Bruichladdich and Bunnahabhain.

Bruichladdich was built in 1881 by Robert, William and John Gourlay Harvey with money from a trust fund set up by their father, William Harvey Jnr. The family had been in the distilling business for some time in the Yoker and Dundashill distilleries in Glasgow. The construction of the distillery and the improvements made to Caol Ila 2 years before were unique in that a newly patented building material, concrete, was being put to one of its first uses on the island.

Bunnahabhain was designed from the start as a high-output malt distillery with a product principally aimed at the blenders in Glasgow. Formed as the Islay Distillery Company in 1881, and incorporated the next year, the partners of this firm spent a great deal of money establishing Bunnahabhain as a premier malt. An entire village grew up around the distillery, complete with schoolhouse and village hall. A link road to the main Bridgend–Port Askaig road was put down as well as a 'commodious and handsome pier at a cost of about £3,500' which was greatly admired by Alfred Barnard. He was also less apprehensive about the approach to Bunnahabhain compared to Caol Ila and clearly felt that the distillery represented the very best in progressive Victorian industrialisation, '. . . this portion of the island was bare, and uninhabited, but the prosecution of the distilling industry has transformed it into a life-like and civilised colony.'

The enclosed-square format of Bunnahabhain's design was reflected in the distillery at Bruichladdich which Barnard entered 'through an archway' into a central courtyard. Not much has changed since — any alterations have been largely within the plant and the external appearance remains the same, although the centrally situated kiln no longer exists and the floor maltings are now silent.

Within a short period, the business of all three distilleries was consolidated. Bulloch, Lade had not only successfully promoted Caol Ila as single bottled malt to compete with the likes of Smith's Glenlivet and Mutter's Bowmore, but had also pushed their BL blend to the top. With the encouragement of W A Robertson of Robertson & Baxter, the partnership operating Bunnahabhain amalgamated in 1887 with W Grant of the Glenrothes-Glenlivet Distillery to form the Highland Distilleries Ltd, and thus increase the group's malt whisky output to 400,000 gallons (1,800,000 litres) per annum. Robertson supported the move by becoming a leading customer. By 1886 the Harvey family had formed the Bruichladdich Distillery Co (Islay Ltd) with a share capital of £24,000 spread amongst five Harveys who then controlled Bruichladdich, Yoker and Dundashill distilleries. The last of these had, for many years, remained the largest pot-still distillery in the Lowlands. Bulloch, Lade's output from Camlachie (by then renamed Loch Katrine) and Caol Ila was in excess of 440,000 gallons (2,000,000 litres) of spirit per year. Throughout the late 1880s, the malt whisky trade enjoyed increased production but this was to change dramatically at the end of the century.

With the increasing consumption of blended whiskies, an aggressive new dimension in marketing took shape. Blenders like Buchanans, Charles Mackinlay & Co, John Walker & Sons Ltd, and Dewars of Perth sold brands abroad with some cunning and great success. Names like the 'Pinch', and Mackie's 'White Horse' were familiar sights at home and overseas. But success adversely affected Bulloch, Lade for a while when demand for their BL brand ran down stocks to the point where the whisky was unavailable.

Blenders started exchanging fillings to satiate the market and new distilleries began to spring up, almost all of them in Speyside. The problems of locality, transport,

*B*ruichladdich's relative youth of just over 100 years explains its more favoured position on Loch Indaal's western shore and the simplicity of its internal layout.

construction costs and distance from the city markets were overriding factors to any blender looking for a suitable site for a new distillery. The modern railway system serving the Highlands made for easy communication with the Lowlands and England and most important of all, the public were beginning to demand a lighter blended whisky, and that meant going to Speyside for malt.

The boom years finally came to an end with the close of the century and the collapse of the Pattisons of Leith in December 1898. Many investors and speculators were left broke in the wake of the scandal which destroyed confidence in the trade in general. The DCL, formed in 1877 as an amalgamation of giant Lowland distilling interests, strengthened their re-solve to safeguard the industry against a repetition of this nature, and embarked upon a programme of rationalisation which formed the basis of the modern industry as it exists today. With distilleries up for sale, and sequestrations commonplace, the DCL moved in, bought up, and closed many of them in an effort to control the industry's output. To this end, the Harveys were approached by the DCL in 1901, during the depression following the Boer War, to sell their Dundashill distillery which had just been converted to patent still operation. They rejected the move and closed the plant, but just 2 years later found themselves firmly in the DCL fold while still retaining control of Bruichladdich. Their interest in the Yoker Distillery had diminished, until it was closed in 1906, leaving them solely with their Islay base.

Meanwhile, a unique relationship had developed between Highland Distilleries and Robertson & Baxter Ltd whereby the distillers marketing was handled by the Glasgow blenders, while remaining in-dependent of each other. Altogether the number of productive distilleries in Scot-land dropped from 161 in 1899 to132 by 1908 whilst the DCL continued to trim the industry – a measure which probably saw it through the First World War. Although the industry responded selflessly to the war effort by switching to the production of industrial alcohols, its contribution was never fully appreciated by a man who, ideally, would have preferred to have seen distilling prohibited – Lloyd George.

Prohibition did occur in 1917, some firms never fully recovering, but the facts of life were explained in a very straight manner to Lloyd George by William Ross of the DCL, and he ditched the more extreme of his proposals for control of alcohol production. Nevertheless, Bulloch, Lade & Co went into voluntary liquidation in 1920 with £½ million of stock in trade, selling out to J P O'Brien Ltd who, on the point of liquidation themselves, immediately turned the company over to a consortium headed by the DCL, Dewars, Watsons of Dundee, W P Lowrie, managed by Robertson & Baxter, and known as the Caol Ila Distillery Co Ltd. The other Bulloch, Lade distilleries at Loch Katrine, and Benmore were sold off, the former to the DCL and the latter to the owners of Lochindaal distillery, Benmore Distilleries, who kept it open until 1927.

By 1922, the effects of prohibition in the United States forced Robertson & Baxter to sell off their entire stocks to Buchanan-Dewar, the DCL and John Walker & Sons, and with the stock went Haig & Haig's revered 'Pinch' brand. Their shares in Caol Ila were taken up by Dewars, John Walker & Sons (who had just entered the consortium), and W P Lowrie. The shares of Watsons of Dundee, who had also just gone into liquidation were disposed of similarly. Any firms within the industry with cash flow problems were realising their assets at this time and invariably it was the DCL and its associates which snapped them up.

This setback did not deter Robertson & Baxter from exploiting the market in the United States through whatever loopholes could be found. Using lines of supply created by the bootleggers, whisky was smuggled into the country from Canada, and the Bahamas. One of Robertson & Baxter's London customers, Berry Bros, managed to find one such line of supply which was to prove invaluable to themselves and their suppliers after the repeal of prohibition in 1933. 'Cutty Sark' was first blended by Robertson & Baxter for Berry Bros in 1923, who actually owned the label (and still do). It was a successful brand from the start, in great demand in the States during prohibition, when any amount of unpalatable hootch was being knocked up in back yards and barns.

Wishing to protect the reputation of their brand, (and no doubt ensure that the discerning American whisky drinker would know exactly what to ask for when prohibition ended) Francis Berry managed to secure the services of one Captain Bill McCoy who was running contraband into the States from Nassau. McCoy had a reputation for dealing only in the genuine article and under his pilotage 'Cutty Sark' remained 'the real McCoy' for thousands of thirsty Americans.

After the amalgamation of Buchanan-Dewar and John Walker with the DCL in 1925 it was inevitable that control of Caol Ila would eventually pass to the parent company. In 1927, the DCL took over after extensive improvements had been made. Management was then passed to the wholly-owned DCL subsidiary, Scottish Malt Distillers, who gained the entire shareholding, worth some £40,000, in 1930. It was then closed immediately, and did not re-open until 1937.

Bruichladdich finally succumbed to the effects of the depression and locked its stills in 1929. However, prohibition in the States had caused Joseph Hobbs to look towards Scotland with a view to supplying the needs of a huge potential market after the repeal, which many people in the industry regarded as inevitable. Hobbs had had mixed fortunes during prohibition, for although he returned to his native Scotland in 1931 having lost money in the Depression (despite being the DCL's Canadian agent for a while), his ship the *Littlehorn* had managed to run over 130,000 cases of Teachers whisky from Antwerp to San Francisco. With his intimate knowledge of the needs of the American whisky drinker, he gained the backing of the National Distillers of America to buy up distilleries through their blenders and

merchants, Train & McIntyre. With his partners Hatim Attari and Alexander Tolmie he bought out the Harveys for £23,000 in 1937 and transferred management to Train & McIntyre's subsidiary, Associated Scottish Distillers. His final tally included Glenury Royal Distillery (1936), Glenlochy (1937), North Esk in Montrose (1938), with Train & McIntyre adding Fettercairn, Benromach and Strathdee in the same year.

Caol Ila was closed again in 1941, followed by Bruichladdich and Bunnahabhain shortly afterwards as a result of wartime restrictions on the amount of grain made available for distilling. Only 44 distilleries were operating in 1942, with most of the produce being shipped across the Atlantic as a valuable Dollar earner for the Government, which continued to raise the duty on spirits for the home market. By 1944, the situation had begun to improve a little, but exports were still the priority, and as soon as distilleries could be recommissioned, they were. Rationing of whisky for the home market forced blenders and distillers to sell their whisky abroad. Malt output rose to over 3.6 million proof gallons (16.3 million litres) in 1944, increasing to almost 6 million gallons (27.2 million litres) the following year when Caol Ila, Bunnahabhain and Bruichladdich were all active again.

Of the three, only Bruichladdich was to see any more changes in ownership to the present day. In 1952, Associated Scottish Distillers sold the distillery to the Glasgow whisky brokers Ross and Coulter. Thus, by chance, once more avoiding the DCL's control who acquired Train & McIntyre in 1953. The increased investment apparent in the 1960s and 70s brought new owners to the distillery – A B Grant's Bruichladdich Proprietors Ltd in 1960 followed by the Invergordon Distillers in 1969, while Bunnahabhain's output was doubled in 1963 with another pair of massive stills. Caol Ila was subjected to a huge reconstruction programme in the early 1970s when SMD demolished the main buildings, bar the magnificent warehouse and in their place erected a 'new distillery which would retain the architectural character of its predecessor...'. That the new structure was bold, there can be no doubt, but the old pagoda roofs and floor maltings which had been such fitting landmarks on the Sound of Islay are sadly missed. Barnard would feel uncomfortable with the modern block of industrial buildings dwarfed by a boiler chimney as they stand today.

By 1975, Invergordon Distillers had enlarged the mash-house and tun room at Bruichladdich without altering the original roofline, which they shared with the stillhouse, to which a new pair of stills was added. With new plant installed, Bruichladdich's potential output approached 800,000 gallons (3.6 million litres) of proof spirit contributing to the formidable total of 5 million gallons (22.7 million litres) which, given the conditions, Islay was capable of producing each year. These conditions have never been present since the expansion of the 1970s, and therein lies the problem of predicting accurately the market demand years in advance and adjusting to meet it. The casual visitor to Caol Ila, Bunnahabhain and Bruichladdich cannot fail to notice that they are not working at full throttle.

The effects of this over-capacity finally manifested themselves on the Sound of Islay in March 1982 when Highland Distilleries closed Bunnahbhain, with the loss of 15 jobs. Six men were kept on to carry out warehousing and maintenance but the atmosphere over the village was soured. Workers were reputedly asked not to talk to the press – a situation for which Highland Distilleries later apologised. The redundant workers stayed on in the company-owned houses with free rent and fuel, the inference being that should production start again, they would be re-employed '...but we can't enter into any commitments...', a company spokesman said at the time.

The malt sector had shrunk from 83.7% of its potential output in 1978 to 38.6% in 1982 and Bunnahbhain alone could have contributed around 4% of this total working at full capacity, but there were 116 other malt distilleries in the same position and closures became a hard, common fact of life. Caol Ila was more fortunate and avoided the DCL closures of early 1983, but lost three men out of a workforce of 23 when, like Lagavulin, it switched to a 4-day week.

Bruichladdich escaped closure until after the 1983 annual shut-down, but had already been working a 5-day week for 2 years as many other independent companies had taken remedial action in advance of the drastic surgery carried out by the DCL. Many industry analysts felt at the time that the closures signified that the worst was over, and the end of a gradual 'period of retrenchment' was in sight. For the workers at Bunnahabhain, the worst was not over until the first week of April 1984 when production was reinstated on a week on/week off basis. This tentative beginning was a reaction to signs of a modest increase in malt whisky consumption at home and abroad. In January 1984 exports of bottled malt whisky increased by 86.5% to 289,000 litres per annum. The DCL made no move to increase production at Caol Ila but the smaller companies were better placed to react and Bruichladdich started producing again in early 1984, continuing until the second week of April when it closed for the annual shut-down.

At the end of the year whisky exports were up by a modest 1% overall, but the malts had advanced by a dramatic 25% overseas. The Italians confirmed their growing taste for malt whisky, buying 51% more than the previous year, making them the largest consumers in the world. Spectacular increases of more than 100% took place in Mexico, Iraq, Brazil and Paraguay, confirming the growing awareness of malt whisky abroad.

It seems unlikely that these distilleries will ever make use of their full production capacity again, but visiting them does at least instil a feeling of confidence in the observer. Almost 100 years after Alfred Barnard had made the same journey, one feels that having survived the very worst, they are in a better position than most to overcome the problems of the 1980s.

BRUICHLADDICH DISTILLERY

BRUICHLADDICH, ISLAY, ARGYLL

Owners:
THE INVERGORDON DISTILLERS LTD
ASHLEY HOUSE
181–195 WEST GEORGE ST
GLASGOW G2 2NL

Licensees:
BRUICHLADDICH DISTILLERY CO LTD

Manager:
IAN ALLAN
Telephone: 049685 221

(Visiting hours are 1400 hrs, Tuesday and Thursday)

At Bridgend, a few miles from Bowmore the road to the 'other side' branches off and skirts the raised beaches around the head of the loch. Sheltered in mature woodland and straddling the River Sorn at a natural ford, the tiny village now consists of a grocery, hotel and a few houses on the bank of the river, but until 1768 was the centre of Islay's commerce. The likely site of David Simson's Killarow distillery is now the veterinary surgery next to the bridge, and the long barn across the road next to the hotel was used as the malting house.

A couple of miles down the A847 from Bridgend, the low whitewashed facade of Bruichladdich Distillery comes into view. Entry is through an attractive wrought iron gate, opening to reveal a spacious and almost totally enclosed courtyard. Ian Allan's offices are on an upper floor above the filling store overlooking the seafront. The floor maltings run the length of the greater part of the front of the distillery, but are at present not being put to any use – although at first sight they would make an excellent reception centre. To the left-hand side of the courtyard, the main processes are carried out. By entering the mash-house to the rear and proceeding along the length of the building, a good understanding of them can be obtained. The beautiful wooden washbacks lie in the next room, followed by the equally attractive stillhouse containing the four stills set square into the raised pine floor

and complemented by the wood-beamed roof. Two spirit safes sitting between the pairs of stills afford the stillman an economy of effort.

What accounts for the relative lightness of Bruichladdich's malt whisky compared to the other Islay whiskies? Harold Currie, formerly of Chivas Bros and S Campbell & Sons Ltd, the Pernod-Ricard subsidiary, brought this up at some of the SWA meetings which he attended. 'The fact that Bruichladdich lies on the western part of Islay means that it is exposed to very subtle differences in climatic and atmospheric conditions compared to the other Islay distilleries. The surrounding flora, fauna and windborne natural yeast will also have an effect, since even on a microscopic scale, malt whisky is the living embodiment of its locality.' No-one disputed what he said since it was, after all, impossible to disprove.

Bruichladdich pier lies a short walk from the distillery. Although it used to serve both Bruichladdich and Port Charlotte distilleries,

the most frequent visitor from the mainland is now the oil tanker offloading the island's supply into the nearby storage tanks. Down at Port Charlotte, a relic from the days of illicit distilling lies in the far corner of the Museum of Islay Life – a small pot still complete with its worm. When it was presented to the Museum's librarian Gordon Booth, the hills behind McArthur's Head were pointed out and he was quietly informed that the still '. . . came from up there.'

Behind the village at Octomore, George Montgomery was distilling during the early part of the 19th Century. This distillery was one of the many established during Walter Frederick Campbell's lairdship after the Small Stills Act of 1816, but it eventually closed after Thomas Pattison quit in 1852. That left the distillery in Port Charlotte, having the better shoreside location, as the only one active in the immediate vicinity. Lochindaal distillery was exactly 100 years old when it was closed by the DCL in 1929 and dismantled. Only the warehouses, now licensed to Macleay Duff (Distillers) Ltd, at the northern end of the village give any indication of that century of activity.

Returning to Bridgend, the A846 is rejoined and leads not only to Bunnahabhain and Caol Ila, but also to the sites of a couple of the other distilleries active in the early 19th Century. As the road rises out of the woods at Bridgend a farm track appears on the right just after the junction on the left for Eallabus (the Islay Estate farm). At the end of the track one finds a well proportioned house in the course of modernisation. But the rearmost outbuilding has a roof reminiscent of a pagoda-topped kiln. Could it have once been a kiln? Possibly, since this is Newton where Neil MacEachern distilled, apparently without a convenient water source – small wonder he didn't stay long. Further up the A846, a right turn at Ballygrant leads behind Loch Ballygrant to Lossit Kennels which used to be the site of Lossit Distillery.

*B*ridgend Distillery, now a veterinary surgery (bottom). Bruichladdich's 'coppers' (right).

TURNBULL GRANT & JACK, ENGINEERS GLASGOW. 1881.

BUNNAHABHAIN DISTILLERY
BUNNAHABHAIN, ISLAY, ARGYLL

Owners and Licensees:
THE HIGHLAND DISTILLERIES PLC
106 WEST NILE STREET
GLASGOW G1 2QY

Manager:
DOUGLAS ECCLES
Telephone: 049684 646

(Although never known to turn anyone
away, it is best to give some prior notice to
either Highland Distilleries or to the
distillery itself.)

The turn-off for Bunnahabhain from the A846 is just a little before the Caol Ila junction as you go from Kiells to Port Askaig. The road down to the distillery is more treacherous than the Caol Ila approach in that it is entirely single-tracked with a number of blind bends. To admire the view up the Sound to Colonsay, it is best to park and not risk meeting a supply lorry trying to catch a ferry for Kennacraig. The road winds past Persabus Farm, Loch nam Ban (Torrabolls Loch, the Caol Ila water supply) and over the top of the cliffs near Rubha a'Mhill, beneath which the rusting hulk of the *Wyre Majestic* lies grounded and rotting since 1974. Far up the Sound, the Rhuvaal lighthouse, built in 1859, gives better warning to those rounding Islay's most northerly point, Rubha a'Mhail.

In April 1984 the SS *Monica*, under a Honduran flag could be seen unloading malt from Eire, the first for 2 years, a sight reminiscent of the earliest days of production at Bunnahabhain, just over a century ago. Then the pier was busy with ships bringing barley from the most unlikely locations. The boom on which Bunnahabhain was built also created shortages in home-grown barley, so a great deal had to be imported. The first ever mash used here was only partly Scottish barley, the remainder came from Poland, Denmark, and Russia.

The enclosed courtyard gives a claustrophobic air to the distillery, but this is more than likely due to the need to conserve ground. Outside the plant, the aspect is much more pleasant, with the ever-present Paps commanding the horizon, and the broad, gentle sweep of the bay creating a welcome contrast to the rugged coastline on either side. Bunnahabhain is the end of the road for the car traveller in this part of Islay, but beyond lies a region of remote beauty open to anybody willing to pack their belongings in a rucksack for a day.

SINGLE MALT SCOTCH WHISKY

The road up the Sound of Islay runs out at Bunnahabhain's gracious bay (far left) where the Wyre Majestic *(above left), rusting on the rocks, guards its southern entrance – as one Islay fisherman commented ". . .probably too much whisky. . ."*

CAOL ILA DISTILLERY
PORT ASKAIG, ISLAY, ARGYLL

Owners:
SCOTTISH MALT DISTILLERS LTD
TRINITY RD ELGIN
IV30 1UF

Licensees:
BULLOCH, LADE & CO LTD
75 HOPE STREET
GLASGOW G2 6AW

Manager:
GRANT CARMICHAEL
Telephone: 049684 207
(Visits to the distillery should be arranged
through SMD at the Elgin office.
Telephone: 0343 7891.)

Caol Ila can only be approached from the A846, where it is clearly signposted just over the back of the hill from Port Askaig. The switchback road descends behind the distillery and runs along the front of the Victorian warehouse, the only remnant of the original block before the rebuilding of the 1970s. In terms of efficiency the programme was a success, with the very latest plant installed and sea water heat exchangers employed to cool the water from the condensers. In all, over £1 million was spent with four new stills added to the original pair in a glass-fronted stillhouse looking out over the Sound to Jura.

Grant Carmichael is always on hand to show visitors round the plant. A tour of the main building quickly familiarises the visitor with all the articles used in a modern distillery of this type. Oregon pine washbacks stand adjacent to the mashtun, both under the supervision of the mashman and brewer, who maintains complete control over the operation from a central console situated on the topmost floor of the mashroom. The massive washbacks are impressive, especially to peer into when empty, but this immaculate room cannot bear comparison to the stillhouse, which is best entered on the uppermost level from the mashroom. A line of six huge gleaming copper stills meets you, their lyne arms stretching back towards the rear of the room creating a dramatic contrast with the scenery viewed through the front of the stillhouse. Despite the intimidating size of the stills, control is again completely centralised from a panel set just behind the middle pair of stills. There can be a few shop floors in Scotland quite like this one.

The offices are set apart from the stillhouse with Grant's poised literally over the sea wall. The 'bay' window aptly describes the view from here. Visitors never leave without being offered a dram of B & L 'Gold Label', or for the fortunate, a rare taste of pure Caol Ila malt, a gesture which fairly improves the outlook on the foulest of days. (The association with Bulloch, Lade was re-established when the distillery was licensed by SMD once more under the name of the firm which had once owned it.) The old warehouse is also visible from here and is gradually being stripped of the awful whitewash which covered its entire surface, revealing a rich red-brick facade.

Caol Ila is built in the next cove to Freeport, where in 1772, Pennant found the miner Freebairn, who had been smelting lead there since 1763. The waterfall behind the distillery which supplies Caol Ila comes from the same source which Freebairn used. These historical associations are hard to imagine against the blatantly modern design of Caol Ila, but despite this it remains one of the most rewarding to visit, not least for its location. One of Islay's other distillery managers described it enviously as 'a cracking distillery.'

Jura lies across the Sound, a short ferry ride away from Port Askaig. This was the major droving halt well into the 19th Century for all the cattle leaving Islay. John MacCulloch aptly described the mayhem that met him when he took the ferry to Feolin in 1824:

*T*HE SHORE WAS COVERED WITH *cattle; and while some were collected in groups under the trees and rocks, crowding to avoid the hot rays of a July evening, others were wading in the sea to shun the flies, some embarking, and another set swimming on shore from the ferry-boats; while the noise of the drovers and the boatmen, and all the bustle and vociferation which whisky did not tend to diminish, were re-echoed from hill to hill, contrasting strangely with the silence and solitude of the surrounding mountains. The disembarkation formed a most extraordinary spectacle. I had seated myself with my back to the horned company, meditating thoughts oblivious of bulls and boats alike, when I was startled by a*

*C*aol Ila (below) and Freeport (above).

plunge under my nose, on which uprose from bottom of the deep a cow, and with such a bound as almost to clear the entire surface. For an instant I forgot myself, and thought it was the very Water Bull of which I had heard. The very long minute that intervened between the plunge of each and its reappearance above the water, as they were all thrown over in succession, was almost awful; and their extreme buoyancy was indicated by the elastic and forcible spring with which they rose above the surface, to fall back again into the sea.

And this was 6 years after the Stent Committee limited the amount of whisky allowed to the ferrymen to a single mutchkin, or ¾ of an English pint for every 30 head of cattle ferried! Before 1818, their allowance was unlimited, and the Stent Committee eventually decided that this was '. . . often injurious to the cattle and the proprietors thereof,' – what about the ferrymen?

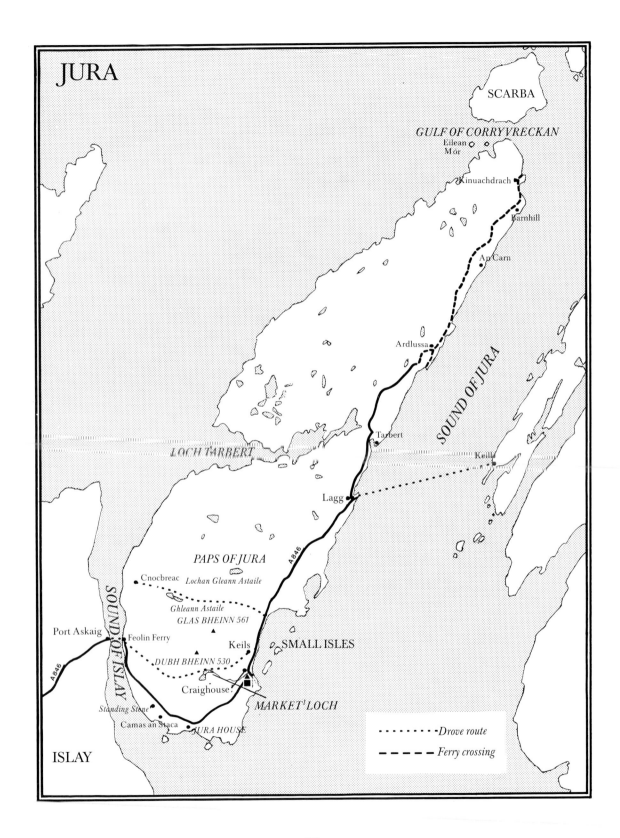

CHAPTER FOUR

JURA

THE FIRST DECADE OF THE 19TH Century brought a contrast in the development of the whisky industry on the mainland and in the islands. The Lowland distillers expanded and increased their output, much to the delight of the Lowland farmers. They were therefore better placed, not only to further increase their share of the massive London market, but also to help satisfy a Government hungry for revenue to support the war against revolutionary France.

After a lengthy review of the industry in 1797, the Government increased the licence fee for a Lowland still to £108 per gallon of still volume. The large, shallow stills which they used enabled a rapid distillation technique to be employed and the licence fee was calculated on the assumption that a Lowland still yielded 2,025 gallons (9,190 litres) of spirit (pretty awful stuff in practice) per gallon of still volume. Any variance above or below this quota resulted in a tax of 3s per gallon – at the same time, weaker washes resulting in better quality spirit were enforced. To cap it all, a duty was imposed on all wash made and all spirit produced while the distillers were still obliged to give 12 months notice to supply the English market.

In the Highlands and Islands the distillers got a different deal with lower taxes imposed on malt prepared from the lower-yielding local barley, the duty on still volume remaining unchanged. Despite these regulations the Lowland distilleries prospered and revenue rose dramatically. A series of appalling harvests precipitated a total ban on distilling in 1801 and 1802, and the decade closed in similar fashion with prohibition from 1809 to 1811. Against this background of hardship, legal distilling on Jura started up in Craighouse around 1810.

At that time, Napoleon's influence on the continent was also having a marked effect on the whisky industry, in that there was an almost constant shortage of imported grain, forcing the more remote distilleries like Jura to rely on modest supplies of local barley. The war also began to have an effect on the drinking habits of the gentry. As brandy became more scarce, whisky grew in popularity but this trend was not apparent in the fortunes of the industry following another rise of duty in 1814.

Prior to 1810 distilling around Craighouse is reputed to have been carried out in a cave until a rudimentary distillery was erected nearby on the site of the present buildings. Local knowledge has it that

David Simson who worked the Bowmore Distillery in the latter part of the 18th Century may have been one of the early distillers at Craighouse before the laird, Archibald Campbell decided to rebuild the operation.

The new buildings included maltings, which helped to produce a characteristic peaty malt whisky – a far cry from the current product. Records show that, in 1831, the first recorded licensee was William Abercrombie, who turned the distillery over to Archibald Fletcher the following year. It then remained in the hands of the Fletchers for the next 20 years.

When Archibald Campbell died in July 1835 his estate passed to his son Colin, who also inherited his father's problems. The estate inventory showed that rent arrears to Martinmas (11 November) 1835 amounted to £2,794 6s 8d, of which £2,245 was deemed 'recoverable'. Peter Fletcher was listed as a tenant in Craighouse and the distillery, then known as the Small Isles, owed £30 for some 20 weeks rent, though this didn't compare with the new laird's financial obligations – he had owed his father over £17,000 when he died.

Money matters apart, Campbell was soon at loggerheads with his Islay counterpart, Walter Frederick just as his father had been. This time the argument was not over the disputed drove roads through southern Jura, but the high levies on the Port Askaig to Feolin ferry, and in 1839 he registered his protest in Court. By the time the Fletchers gave up the lease of the distillery, there were only 1,200 gallons (5,450 litres) of malt whisky in bond on the island and its reputation appeared to have been in question. In December 1851, the factor Neil MacLeod wrote to Richard Campbell who had succeeded Colin to the estate: *As I was leaving the Small Isles, [he] gave me a sample of his best aged whisky, which I have seen compared at Portaskaig with Caol Ila by the manager Mr Dain, who I believe knows the business well, and makes the best aqua in Islay. I could not get him to express himself as to whether Jura could be improved or not, he merely said, old or new it retained its former taste. I believe on the whole the whisky is rather better . . .*

The distillery passed into the hands of J and A Gardner (or Gardinner) in 1852, but almost immediately there were problems. The Gardners quit, leaving Campbell with the option of selling off the plant for scrap, or finding another distiller who was prepared to take over production at such short notice. Valuations on the brass and copper content of the plant amounted to £400, with the entire contents of the distillery coming to £600, but the valuator felt that realistically only £400 could be raised if it was all sold for its intended purpose. The dilemma was resolved when Campbell was approached by Norman Buchanan of Glasgow, and after some customary haggling a lease was agreed at £90 per annum for 5 years and £110 per annum thereafter. This included the 'use of the utensils', with the tenant compensating for any reduction in their value at the end of the lease. The laird agreed to supply Buchanan with all the peat he required and assurances were given that all the draff would be taken up by farmers on Jura and Islay.

Buchanan entered the distillery in April 1853, around the same time he took over Caol Ila distillery, which, despite its reputation had been without a licensee since Henderson, Lamont & Co had gone bust the previous year. Ten years later Buchanan's business went the same way and the next operators of Jura distillery were J & K Orr from 1867–1872. Only in 1876, when James Ferguson and Sons of Cadogan St, Glasgow took over, did Jura enter a period of relative stability, although it was ultimately to end in acrimony between tenant and laird.

Richard Campbell's estate passed to James Campbell who arranged a lease for 34 years from Whitsunday 1884 in which he made sure that the new tenants of the distillery undertook to improve the facilities at Craighouse. He did this by binding them 'at their own cost and expense, to erect and completely finish a good substantial pier, with a depth of not less than ten feet of water at the pier head at low water,' and to 'erect a waiting-room and store on the pier, with road access sufficiently wide to allow two loaded carts to pass at any point,' and a bridge wide enough to take one cart.

The Fergusons must have sunk a considerable amount of money into Jura – the improvements to the distillery alone cost some £25,000. This accounted for four washbacks of 13,000 gallons (59,000 litres) each, a 6,650-gallon (31,200-litre) wash still, two spirit stills of 2,350 and 1,200 gallons (10,670 and 5,450 litres) capacity producing 180,000 gallons (817,200 litres) of spirit per annum.

In 1901, James Campbell died and was succeeded by his son Colin. At the same time the Fergusons quit Jura distillery, stripping it of all the plant and machinery which they had installed at the start of their tenancy. Their reasons for leaving are obscure, but most sources feel that they were in dispute with the laird. Some correspondence of 1895 between James Ferguson and James Campbell concerns fencing which had been erected by Campbell around the distillery and road-way down to the pier, which Ferguson described as 'at best useless', beseeching him to take it down.

The bonded whisky was removed gradually to the mainland, and in 1905 there was sufficient need for an Excise officer's house to be built at a cost of £869 8s 7d. The Fergusons continued to pay rent up to the expiry of the lease at Whitsunday 1918 when the pier, access road and bridge became the property of the laird. By this time the Fergusons had more or less washed their hands of their interests on the island. The last whisky had left for the mainland in 1913 and they had not bothered to pay much heed to the upkeep of the pier – at least according to Campbell.

Prior to the expiry Campbell had a survey of the pier carried out by G Woulfe Brenan of Oban who set the extent of the repairs at £1,293. The Fergusons felt that £67 was closer to the mark and the stage was set for another confrontation.

The Fergusons steadfastly refused to pay for the repairs and in October 1920, Campbell instigated legal proceedings against them only to find that George Ferguson had been dead for some time, and James Ferguson was to die soon after the action was served. Upset with the whole affair, Campbell had the roofs removed from the distillery buildings to avoid paying the rates on them and pursued the Ferguson's Trustees. In December 1920 he sued them for £2,793, which included £1,000 for the dredging of the pierhead, where the water depth Campbell claimed, was less than 10 feet at the termination of the lease. If this argument was ever resolved, no record of it was made, but the Fergusons had a very belligerent attitude to the whole affair and were clearly in no mood to settle. In any case, distilling as a viable industry was, for the time being, finished on Jura.

The reasons for the reconstruction of Jura's distillery in the early 1960s are, thankfully, better recorded. As an island, Jura was subjected to the social and economic pressures common to any isolated community. Both war and the drift of the young to the industrial heartlands had reduced the population to around 150 in the late 1950s. Visitors to the island were usually there to stalk the deer which existed in their thousands. George Orwell commented bitterly on the 'deer forest' during his stay at Barnhill in the north of the island. The way in which 'everything is sacrificed to the brutes' did not impress him.

It was Orwell's landlord, Robin Fletcher, along with Mr Riley-Smith, the owner of Jura estate in the south of the island, who responded to the worsening situation by embarking on an ambitious plan to rebuild the distillery at Craighouse, in the hope that new blood would be attracted to the island. They recruited Delmé-Evans, who had designed and built Tullibardine distillery in 1947-48, and gave him free rein over the design. Even Delmé-Evans followed in the island mould as a farmer and distiller, and with a thorough understanding of the value of limited ground, he set about putting the hillside site to the best possible use. There was no constraint placed on the type of whisky which he wanted to create and at the outset a Highland-type malt was envisaged to set itself apart from the heavier, highly-peated neighbouring Islay malts.

'My primary aim was to construct an economic distillery within the space available,' Delmé-Evans recalls. 'Everything had to be simple and fall to hand. You could not afford to complicate things in so remote a location. I also had to play mother the large number of incomers on an island without any policemen – some Saturday nights became quite interesting!' The original concept was for 250,000 gallons (1.14 million litres) per year from two stills, the design of which was crucial to the taste of the new Jura malt. 'It was our intention to produce a Highland-type malt differing from the typically peaty stuff last produced in 1900. I therefore designed the stills to give spirit of a Highland character, and we ordered malt which was only lightly peated.'

The weather was a factor over which Delmé-Evans had no control, so the boats bringing plant and machinery to Craighouse were frequently delayed. The *Lochard* was often employed on these supply runs but was restricted by having

OLD JURA DISTILLERY

*T*he floor maltings before they were razed (left). The manager's house (above) can be seen on the right and still stands.

The old buildings, excepting the manager's quarters and the earthen-floored cooperage were razed as an imported 230-strong labour force moved into the area in 1960. Through the determined efforts of Robin Fletcher, Jura was finally connected to the National Grid by cable laid from Kiells on the Argyll shore – an invaluable 'bonus' for the builders and something which may have taken considerably longer to happen in normal circumstances. Until then, Jura had relied on locally-generated electricity from water-driven turbines installed in 1910. He also helped to raise financial backing for the project from Scottish Brewers whose wine and spirits subsidiary, the Waverley Group, now holds a 72% shareholding in the company. Sadly, before construction began, Robin Fletcher died leaving the other partners to see the job through. It was largely his hard work in the preparation of the project which enabled them to complete it in 3 years.

only a 10-ton lifting derrick and much of the plant had therefore to be brought over in sections and built up on site.

Starting up a distillery involves an element of risk, since the quality of the malt whisky can only be discovered when it has matured. In Jura's case the risks were lessened simply due to the fact that the water supply was of known quality, so the most essential ingredient was right from the start. Today's commercial distillers can order top quality malted barley to their precise specifications and along with controlled mashing and fermentation the only real unknowns are the water and the shape of the stills. In 1968, Delmé-Evans had seen another of his creations come on stream – the Glenallachie Distillery on Speyside, 'but it had taken me 3 years on my own to find a suitable water source.' Jura's water came from the trusted Loch a'Bhaile Mhargaidh (Market Loch) lying at 800 feet (244 metres) in the hills behind Craighouse.

The distillery was opened by Lord Polwarth of the Scottish Council on the April 26th 1963, and became a major employer on the island. Many of the workforce were recruited from the mainland and encouraged to settle in Craighouse, but inevitably some could not reconcile themselves to the island way of life and left Jura after a while. However, the belief that the distillery would inject new life into the island and bring about an increase in the population proved to be correct – it gradually increased to the present level of around 250, 11 of whom are employed in the distillery.

Delmé-Evans witnessed this increase as Managing Director of the distillery company until 1975, when he retired. The company was by then economically sound enough to undertake a self-financing expansion programme over the next 3 years. In 1976, under the new MD, Dr Alan Rutherford and his manager Don Raitt (now at Ardbeg), the new boilerhouse was built and the old gravity feed system in the filling store replaced with a more modern pneumatic type, which now performs the job in much the same way as a petrol pump. The following year, the stillhouse was extended with another pair of stills, new condensers, feints receiver and spirit safe. A 20-ton wet draff tank was installed along with a new draff drier designed to handle all the draff produced at a projected output of 750,000 gallons (3.4 million litres) per year.

Building of a new dam at Market Loch was started in 1977, but after several unsuccessful attempts to get materials up to the loch by Land-Rover, the work was put off until the next year when a helicopter solved the problem. The final push to complete the programme involved the raising of the tun room roof and installation of a centralised electrical control system for the mash-house and tun room.

The old cast iron mash tun was dismantled and removed, being replaced by a 20-foot diameter stainless steel lauter tun, in order to increase the efficiency of the mashing. The six corten steel washbacks, which became subject to pitting after prolonged use, were also replaced with stainless steel versions of double the capacity. An important addition to the cleansing equipment was the installation of an in-house flushing system utilising all the existing pipework to wash out the tun, liquor tanks and washbacks after use. Further plant was renewed with a large oak spirit receiver from Marchive Fruhinsolz of Jarnac, France, installed by Joseph Brown of Dufftown and the malt intake was increased to 30 tons per hour.

Did all these improvements make a better distillery? A more prolific one certainly, but only when everything is working properly which, as the manager John Bulman will agree, does not happen all the time. Something of the simplicity which Delmé-Evans built into the original plan has gone, even though the distillery operates on two men per shift. The result is that John has become a jack of all trades, having had to sort out all sorts of teething troubles to get Jura operating consistently, but that is something of which Delmé-Evans as a farmer, architect and distiller would approve.

*J*ura Distillery (top) overlooking Small Isles Bay which was the name of the distilling operation which existed in the same place until 1901 when the Fergusons quit in a dispute with the laird James Campbell. The present distillery produces a refreshingly Highland type of malt whisky. Barnhill (above), where George Orwell wrote 1984 and where his tuberculosis, from which he was eventually to die, gradually worsened. The house is still owned by Margaret Nelson, who was formerly married to Robin Fletcher. The Corryvreckan seen from An Cruachan (right) looking over to Scarba's south-eastern corner. At times like this, when the waters are calm, it seems idyllic, but its whirlpool has claimed many ships — it nearly claimed George Orwell!

JURA DISTILLERY

CRAIGHOUSE, ISLE OF JURA, ARGYLL

Owners and Licensees:
ISLE OF JURA DISTILLERY CO LTD

Manager:
JOHN BULMAN
Telephone: 049682 240

Normally the traveller to Jura will arrive from Port Askaig on the *Isle of Gigha* in full view of the Paps dominating the heart of the island. More often than not they remain shrouded in mist and hill cloud, giving the mistaken impression that Jura is bereft of high ground, but during the fairer summer months the shimmering quartzite peaks are a familiar sight from both Islay and deep into the mainland. The single track road from Feolin follows the same path as the one constructed largely at Archibald Campbell's expense during the first decade of the 19th Century and carried through to Lagg in an effort to improve communications.

Campbell of Jura disputed Walter Frederick Campbell's right to use the new and easier coastal route as a drove road for his cattle, insisting that he had the right to use only the old routes over the higher ground. These old drove roads are to be found to the north of the present road, and are attractive to hillwalkers wishing to approach Craighouse as the drovers did in the 18th and 19th Centuries. The more northerly route starts at Cnocbreac and follows the burn up to Lochan Gleann Astaile, passing between the most southerly of the Paps, Beinn a'Choalais (734 metres), and Glas Bheinn (561 metres) and rising to a height of about 300 metres before descending to Jura Forest and Small Isles Bay.

The more common route was from Feolin, where the cattle landed from Port Askaig, over the lower flank of Dubh Bheinn (530 metres) to Market Loch, which supplies the distillery. The cattle were then taken down to the coast near Kiels and on up to Lagg, where they were ferried over to Kiells on the Argyll coast.

One of Thomas Telford's engineers, Joseph Mitchell, who carried out a great deal of work in the Highlands and Islands on harbours and railways, once made the crossing from the mainland in appalling conditions:

*O*N ARRIVING AT THE FERRY, *we found every corner of the inn crowded with drovers who had been detained by the weather for several days, and were passing their time, as was their wont, in riotous and continuous drinking . . . .*

We appealed to the ferrymen to take us across. At first they positively refused on account of the storm, but with some persuasion, and a handsome douceur, their scruples were overcome, and they prepared for the voyage.

No sooner had the drovers, who had been so long detained, heard that the boat was to cross at our instigation, than they got excessively angry, talked in Gaelic long and loud, and insisted that we should take at the same time a cargo of their cattle. This the boatmen could not refuse, and

eighteen cattle were put on board . . .

At last we cleared the land, and got into the channel. How the wind did roar, and how the cattle struggled to get their heads free! The extent of sail we carried was forcing the bow of the boat too deep into the sea, and there was fear of being swamped.

The men tried to lower the sail, which, in their agitation, they could not effect, and all looked helpless.

On this the drover seized the helm, and with sharp and decisive words took the command of the boat . . .

We had to take the narrow and rocky entrance of Lagg harbour, a most difficult navigation; but the drover's sharp and distinct orders were promptly obeyed, and in no time he landed us in shelter within the little bay . . .

The time we took to effect the crossing, nine miles, was little more than half an hour.

After being shipped to the mainland, the cattle continued over established drove roads to the markets of Stirling and Falkirk.

The coast road (A846) from Feolin is naturally much kinder, rounding the south of the island past the standing stone at Camas an Staca Jura House, the home of Mr Riley-Smith, and the forestry plantation at Sannaig, before dropping into Craighouse. John Bulman, the manager, is always pleased to have visitors at Jura and show them round. His assistant manager Willie Tait is also available to act as guide and dispense the generous drams in the office afterwards. Jura is something of which Delmé-Evans can be justly proud, both as a distillery and as a single malt. As a lighter, more fragrant dram than the Islay malts, it has fulfilled its creator's hopes and Jura's commercial success with both the public and the blenders speaks for itself.

Although Jura distillery can be explored on a day trip from Islay, the island itself is

worth more time and the Jura Hotel at Craighouse serves as the best base for visitors. The A846, which passes between the distillery and the hotel carries on up the eastern side of the island through the Astor's estate at Tarbert to Lagg, and from there to Ardlussa which was Robin Fletcher's home. Beyond Ardlussa, the road is impassable to the majority of vehicles – George Orwell used a battered motorcycle when he first travelled this road on his way to Barnhill in the north of the island to write *1984*. The locals are bemused, and a little surprised by the number of 'Orwell Hunters' who have trekked to the remote farmhouse, particularly in 1984 itself. To those who knew him he was simply Mr Blair, a slightly reclusive but 'very nice man'. He was fond of his dram as well, as his brother-in-law, Bill Dunn recalls. 'It was usually Lamb's Navy rum, gin or brandy, but everything was rationed then so it was all pretty hard to come by.' Although alcohol was scarce, he managed to get whisky from his friend Richard Rees when he visited occasionally. He also had the sense not to bother repeating his disastrous experiments while a teacher in Southwold, trying to distil alcohol from treacle.

Bill Dunn observed Orwell for longer than most, and relates a story which sums up the Orwell who was greatly attached to the English country life, and attempted to create a level of self-sufficiency (albeit a semblance) at Barnhill. Orwell had brought his woodworking tools with him when he moved to Jura, but his execution of the craft was never really as great as his enthusiasm for it. Bill was out scything and raking hay one day in the summer of 1948 when the shaft of his rake broke, so he made his way down to Barnhill to see if he could leave the rake with Orwell. Orwell insisted that he could fix the rake on the spot and had Bill follow him into the workshop. 'Orwell became very pensive and looked at the broken pieces this way and that, until after a few minutes he mused, "mmm, yes . . . copper nails, I think."

The neighbouring farm of Kinuachdrach, the site of the most northerly change-house on Jura, lies between Barnhill and the Gulf of Corryvreckan, which has gained a reputation far more fearsome than it

*J*ura's 'long road' (left) follows its eastern shore as far as Ardlussa (bottom), home of the Fletchers. Thereafter it deteriorates and continues to Kinuachdrach (below), Jura's deer (far right) ever-present.

deserves. In 1792, the Reverend Francis Stewart had this to say of the channel in the Old Statistical Account of Scotland: *THE famous Gulf of Breacan lies between Jura and Scarba. The sound between these two islands is narrow, and forming a communication between the Atlantic and the internal sea on the coast of Argyll; the rapidity and violence of tides are tremendous. The gulf is most awful with the flowing tide; in stormy weather, with that tide, it exhibits an aspect, in which a great deal of the terrible is blended. Vast openings are formed, in which one would think the bottom might be seen; immense bodies of water tumble headlong, as over a precipice, then rebounding from the abyss, meet the torrents from above; they dash together with inconceivable impetuosity, rise foaming to a prodigious height above the surface: the noise of their conflict is heard through the surrounding islands. This gulf is an object of as great terror to the modern, as Sylla and Charybdis were to the ancient mariners. It is industriously avoided by all who navigate these sounds: there are instances, however, of vessels being drawn into it. Large stout vessels make their way through it in its greatest rage, but to small craft it proves immediate destruction.*

To put this account into perspective, Orwell very nearly came to grief while out on a boating trip with his nephew, niece, and adopted son Richard, in 1947. It appears he had misread the tide tables, and ended up being rescued by a fishing boat, having been lucky enough to land on Eilean Mór. Curiously, he was completely unperturbed by the experience. On the other hand, Bill Dunn swam the gulf in 1981 to raise money for the disabled at the time when the waters were at their calmest, that is, not in flood. Bill, who lost one of his legs in World War II succeeded where many other 'small craft' have failed.

The trek to the north of Jura to view the Corryvreckan in flood from An Cruachan is well worth the time and effort, particularly in the summer months. It is wise to give the turbulent waters a wide berth on the passage north to Mull. Moving up the Sound of Luing, Scarba and the Garvellach Isles, pass on the port side with the lusher and more fertile Luing to starboard. The drab, slate

quarries of Easdale soon loom up as the tiny island of Balnahua materialises like a satanic tombstone about a mile offshore. When Hugh Miller, the 19th Century geologist, sailed past in the *Betsey* he was able to watch the quarrymen working the deposits on the Easdale shore. Incredibly, the tiny chip of Balnahua supported a thriving slate-quarrying community in the 18th and 19th Centuries of some 150 people. Now, the only visible signs of habitation are the naked gable ends of the numerous ruined cottages. South of Kerrera island, which covers

Oban Bay, lies Puilldhobrain (Pool of the Otter). King Haco's expedition of 1263 is known to have been in this area before pressing south to unsuccessfully settle accounts with the Scottish Crown at the Battle of Largs, and Puilldhobrain would appear to have been their most likely anchorage.

Crossing from here to Mull one passes to the south of Lismore of which the shrewd John MacCulloch had this to say: *THE fertility of Lismore in grain, renders it a centre of illicit distillation, for which the facilities are also greatly increased by its extent of sea coast, and the consequent ease with which the manufactured commodity can be exported; while the vicinity and population of all the surrounding shores, offer a ready market for the sale of the produce.*

Beyond, at the mouth of the Sound of Mull stands that most striking of island fortresses, the home of the MacLeans – Duart Castle.

CHAPTER FIVE

MULL

BOWMORE'S CREATION AS A purpose-built village was reflected in 1788 when Tobermory was established on the shores of 'one of the best natural harbours in Great Britain . . .', as reported by John Knox in 1786 to the subscribers of the British Society for Promoting the Fisheries of Scotland. The Society was formed to establish fishing communities on the west coast and to exploit the vast stocks of herring, cod, ling and salmon which lay offshore.

Knox went on a fact finding mission to reconnoitre possible sites for these communities and submitted his observations to the Society, which consisted, incidentally, largely of west-coast landowners and other men of substance. The governor, needless to say, was the omnipresent Duke of Argyll, who happened to own a great deal of Mull.

Knox was an enthusiastic but somewhat naive observer and was none too impressed by the farming standards he witnessed on his journey north to Mull: *Of grain, this coast cannot raise, with the greatest exertions, a sufficiency for the use of the inhabitants; and of every year's production of*

The Sound of Mull provides an exciting sailing ground for the keen yachtsman, with stunning views of the mountains of Mull, dark and massive, lying behind the village of Salen.

Barley, a third or fourth part is distilled into a spirit called whisky, of which the natives are immoderately fond.

He arrived in Oban and found that his transport to Mull had not materialised, but he was fortunate to befriend . . . 'Two brothers, of the name Stevenson, who are traders in that place, and to whose industry, that whole district is under great obligations . . .', who, 'seeing my situation, readily offered to accompany me up the Sound, in a new vessel of their own, lying in the bay.'

The offer of a lift up the Sound of Mull was to prove invaluable to the Stevensons who must have impressed upon Knox their ability to be of use to the Society in the future construction of any settlements in the area. Meanwhile Knox recorded that, 'There is not, in this large island, any appearance of a regular well built village, or of manufactures or even spinning to any extent.'

The sheltered bay of Tobermory made a big impression on him, however, and he even went on to suggest to the Duke of Argyll that, 'docks might be formed for building Ships of War. This harbour might indeed be employed by government as an Arsenal for the facilitating of naval equipments and military embarkations in Time of War for America and the West Indies.'

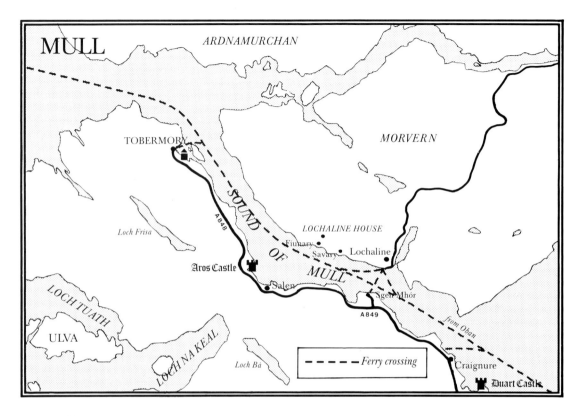

In his submission to the Society, Knox proposed that 40 fishing stations should be established along the west coast. These stations would ideally consist of 16 houses for tradesmen, schoolmaster and innkeeper, erected at a cost of £80 each and 20 houses for the fishermen, at a less substantial cost of £25 – in other words, single story and thatched, as opposed to two stories and slated. His oversimplified calculations added up to £80,000 being expended on the entire 40 stations. The Secretary of the Society, John Mackenzie, criticised Knox's assumption that so many stations could be established and remain commercially viable and the decision was eventually taken to establish four stations at Tobermory, Ullapool, Lochbay and Creich.

The Duke expected some '30 years purchase of the present rent' for Tobermory from the Society which placed advertisements in leading journals for tradesmen and fishermen to petition them for situations in the new villages. This democratic gesture was somewhat tempered by the Duke's guidelines to the Society's agent (and his own factor) on Mull, James Maxwell, to whom he wrote in May 1788:

*I*N FIXING SETTLERS I WOULD *have you privately give some attention and preference to such as are considered friendly to my family, but not to the exclusion of any person of real merit whatever they may be in other respects . . .*

Adding that on Mull he had been approached by a smith and a carpenter with offers for rentals, and that 'they had good characters, one of them was a Campbell.'

This reference on behalf of his namesake was proffered despite his continuing: *N*O ARTIFICIER SHOULD BE *settled unless known good workmen and persons of good character: such as have been bred in Mull or such remote places, unless of some extraordinary merit should not be accepted.*

Construction started in 1788 with much of

the work being carried out by Knox's acquaintance John Stevenson of Oban who was responsible for the breastwork built along the high water mark. The Stevensons later became involved in distilling when they established the Oban distillery around 1794. When the family were finally forced out of business in 1829 they had not only created markets down the coast into England, which they supplied with a small fleet of three steam boats, but were also involved in the slate quarries at Balnahua!

The tenants started to move in as their houses rose around them and by 1792 the customs-house was established to cope with the traffic Tobermory was then handling. Between April 5th and October 10th 1792, some 1,829 tons of kelp, mostly bound for the glass and soap factories of Greenock and Liverpool, were cleared for export, along with 1,070 tons of British salt, 15 tons of lead, 120 cwt of wool, 53 barrels of herring, 17½ barrels of salmon, and 46 cwt of cod and ling. At the same time 1,066 gallons (4,840 litres) of wine, 3,575¼ gallons (16,232 litres) of 'British spirituous liquors' and 659½ gallons (2,994 litres) of the foreign variety (ie brandy, claret, and genever) entered the port.

At this time two licensed stills existed within the parish, already well supplied by the imported spirits.

The Wash Act of 1784 obliged distillers to take out a licence, and prohibited more than two stills operating in a parish at any one time while restricting the amount of barley consumed for this purpose to 250 bolls per still. No sign of any such distilling within the village (now with a population of some 300 people) was apparent, although the local minister had observed much activity outwith Tobermory, reporting that until: *T*HE LATE ACT . . . THE *manufacturing of barley into whisky, was by much too common a practice in this country; but the number of stills have, since that period, been greatly diminished, much to the advantage of the country, and, it is thought, without any loss to the revenue.*

The village was growing steadily – the rent rolls show that the boatbuilder and cooper shared a shed rent free, while a smith, a wright and various other tradesmen had taken up lots. Another tenant was John Sinclair, a merchant, taking several rentals over a number of years and applying in April 1797 to the society: *T*O TAKE A LEASE *for 57 years of 80 feet in front and 90 feet backwards of vacant ground at Ledaig. To build stone and lime houses on the front ground and office houses on the back ground, and to make a cut from the Burn or River. As Mr Maxwell thinks the Society cannot alienate so much ground below the bank (Mr Sinclair) is willing to renounce the lease after 10 years possession at 12 months notice . . . (Mr Sinclair) will build (at a cost) not exceeding £300 . . . (and) expects grass for a horse and moss for two fires.*

Although the word 'distillery' at no time appears, the Society's answer on May 16th showed that they had clearly discerned Sinclair's intentions: *D*ECLINES PROPOSAL *of John Sinclair for erecting a distillery at Tobermory. If it will suit Mr Sinclair to erect a brewery the Society would second that idea more readily.*

This proved to be only a temporary setback for Sinclair who was establishing himself as the settlers' spokesman. Sometime in 1798 the Society gave in to his request and he built his distillery. There appears to be no record of how he changed the Society's mind, although in his original offer he mentioned that he would 'provide the fish cures with a sufficient cellar for containing salt.' Perhaps he eventually made them an offer they could not refuse.

In his first year of operation he produced 292 gallons (1,326 litres) of spirit from stills which by law had to be between 30 and 40 gallons (136 and 182 litres) in volume, so he clearly maintained his still as a secondary occupation to that of merchant.

His grain supplies would almost certainly have come in from surrounding districts or by import, for the ground surrounding Tobermory was extremely barren and much of the Society's correspondence at this time dealt with requests for extra pasturage from settlers who universally complained of the rent. Eventually in 1801, the Duke of Argyll took a rental from MacLean of Duart for the tack of Calve Farm, which included Calve Island at the mouth of Tobermory bay, to alleviate the problem. Some 18 sublets were then created for tenants, one of whom inevitably, was John Sinclair.

He never seems to have missed an opportunity to consolidate his business in Tobermory. He had a fleet of trading ships working between Glasgow and Liverpool, no doubt carrying a great deal of the kelp produced in the isles and he even managed to issue his own local currency. His notes bore the following promise: *T*OBERMORY, *Island of Mull, 9th January, 1825. For want of change, I owe you five shillings and for four of these tickets I will give you a £1 note – John Sinclair.*

The authorities took a rather dim view of all this for in 1826 the promissories were mentioned in evidence before the Small Note Commission. Since 1765 it had in fact been illegal to issue notes of less than 20 shillings value and the fine for such an offence was £500.

Even if Sinclair was fined, he was well enough able to pay, since he had in fact retired in 1813 at the age of 43, having made a considerable fortune in the district. He had married into an old Argyll family, the MacLachlans of Rahoy, and started to build up a large estate on the Morvern peninsula around Lochaline. The Argyll Estate sale of 1813 allowed him to purchase the farms of Achnaha, Achabeg, Keil and Knock for £10,000, adding Fiunary, Savary, Achafors and Kinlochaline a few years later. The result being the 8,550 acre Lochaline Estate for the sum total of £20,000, or £2 6s 10d per acre.

Lacking only a residence in which to settle his family he commenced building Lochaline House in 1821, but as it neared completion 4 years later his wife Catherine died suddenly. With five children to bring up, he concentrated his efforts solely on

their welfare and the improvement of his estate and his tenants' well-being. Following his wife's death, he withdrew from the distillery. With Sinclair's passing, much of the early history concerning the distillery goes too. A succession of licensees over the early 19th Century preceded the distillery's closure in 1837, for reasons that are none too clear.

Sinclair continued to live at Lochaline until his death in January 1863 from old age and debility. He had been a generous and philanthropic laird who had never turned anyone from his door and his passing caused great concern in the parish. His grand-daughter Agnes King recorded in 1902: *T*HE DEPARTURE OF THE FAMILY *from the house which had been for so long a blessing to the whole district, was a source of*

*T*obermory . . .it seems not to have grown piecemeal, as a village ought, but to have been made wholesale, as Frankenstein made his man; and to be ever asking, and never more incessantly than when it is at its quietest, why it should have been made at all?

Hugh Miller

distress and lamentation to all, but especially to the poor, to whom it had constantly been an open door of escape in time of need, for none were sent away without comfort to mind and body. I cannot forget one old man on the day we left, weeping as he wrung his hands, saying, 'Morvern is a widow today.' In the Gaelic language many of them expressed their sorrow to Mother in words untranslatable – so full of anguish were they – in that most expressive of all languages.

The distillery had gradually fallen into disuse and was entered by John Clark Jnr and Partners of Glasgow after their bobbin manufactory in Salen had burnt down in 1855. They moved the plant machinery up the Sound to the distillery where it was stored until it could be set up, but in 1861 two Glaswegian scrap dealers, Duncan Macfarlane and Daniel Murray, broke into the building in an unsuccessful attempt to remove the machinery.

Not until 1878 was the distillery at Ledaig re-established, changing hands twice during the latter part of the century until John Hopkins & Co took over the licence in 1890. The DCL bought them out in 1916, allowing the distillery to operate under the same name, which is still clearly visible on the gable end of the warehouse overlooking the distillery. Then, in June 1930, like a great many other distilleries, it was closed and remained silent until 1972.

It still had its uses though, and during World War II the large warehouse was used for Naval Stores as John Knox's vision of a Navy base at Tobermory became an eventual reality. Some 800 sailors under Vice Admiral Stevenson were harboured in the bay with 200 allowed ashore at any one time. The distillery itself was used as the canteen for a maximum of six ships, while the *Western Isles* lay permanently in the bay serving as accommodation.

Part of the roadside premises has for a long time been used by the Hydro Board as an electricity generating plant – this has not helped the problem of good access to the plant. It was eventually purchased from the DCL and re-opened in 1972 as the Ledaig Distillery Ltd, by a consortium representing Liverpool shippers, later joined by the Domecq sherry group from Spain. The distillery was extensively reconstructed between 1970 and 1972 with output being raised from 350,000 gallons (1.59 million litres) to 800,000 gallons (3.63 million litres).

This doubling of capacity was unfortunately to be a major factor in the eventual collapse of the firm in 1975, since it was coupled with the fact that the company had only one major customer who sought other supplies.

The receiver was appointed in 1976 and discharged 3 years later by the Kirkleavington Property Company, which had no previous interests in distilling. Under Tobermory Distillers Ltd, production in 1979 ran to 42 hogsheads (around 6,510 litres) increasing to 575 hogsheads the following year. Sadly Tobermory has not produced since, and realistically is unlikely ever to do so again. Although a blended whisky has been available under the Tobermory label since August 1980, sales have been largely to the local tourist trade and Tobermory malt has never gained the steadfast reputation within the industry which is enjoyed by the other island malts.

Stock of the blend ran out at the distillery in February 1985, just two months before the manager Alan Jappy and the rest of his staff were made redundant. Efforts to sell the distillery since the Autumn of 1983 have come to nothing, and although production was planned to start up again in April 1984, this too was cancelled.

Tobermory's problems were that it not only produced spirit inefficiently but also suffered from poor design, having two tun rooms on opposite sides of the plant, and no facility for in-house cleansing as exists at Jura. Had these modifications been integrated into a properly designed plant during the reconstruction of 1970–72, then Tobermory might yet be producing. Instead, with its warehouse nearly emptied of stock and its doors bricked up to avoid the rates burden, it may soon deteriorate to the point where it becomes nothing more than a museum piece for the summer tourists.

*T*obemory Distillery occupies the ground by the Ledaig burn on the foreshore of the spacious and picturesque harbour. The lack of available ground for warehousing probably compounded the problems which eventually led to the closure of the distillery. There is little chance of Tobermory producing malt whisky again in the foreseeable future.

TOBERMORY DISTILLERY
TOBERMORY, ISLE OF MULL, ARGYLL

Owners & Licensees:
TOBERMORY DISTILLERS LTD

ST JOHN'S PLACE
CLECKHEATON
WEST YORKSHIRE BD19 3RR

Manager:
NONE

Telephone: 0274 873351

Duart Castle is blessed with one of the most prominent situations of all the island castles. It was restored in the early 20th Century as a family home by Sir Fitzroy MacLean, the father of the current chief, and signals the start of the journey up the Sound of Mull to Tobermory.

On the way up the Sound, the ruins of John Sinclair's mansion house lie embedded in woodland, a few miles to the west of Lochaline. The Sound turns north-west at Salen leading naturally to Tobermory, which emerges from behind the shelter of Calve Island, as the terraced houses high on the hill above the harbour come into view.

It is easy to see why Tobermory's harbour has for so long been considered one of the best on the west coast – surrounded by high ground and protected from the swell by Calve Island, it is near perfect for ship and yacht alike, although Sam Johnson did note in 1773 that '. . . there is a hollow between the mountains, through which the wind issues from the land with very mischievious violence.' Since then trees and town have blended to create a more secure atmosphere, which is enhanced in the evening as the lights of the town seduce the yachtsman into the pubs ashore.

Yachtsmen must row ashore in Tobermory, perhaps over the body of the Spanish galleon *Florida*, lying on the floor of the harbour since 1588 when she mysteriously exploded having fled northwards after the defeat of the Armada. Most visitors, however, come off the Oban ferry at Craignure and take the bus or drive up to Tobermory. Remarkably, the town's pier has not been employed by Caledonian MacBrayne for some time, but a recent Scottish Office directive from George Younger, the Secretary of State for Scotland, means that the pier will soon be restored and the ferry will again berth at the opposite end of the harbour from the distillery.

Once inside the central courtyard of the distillery, the extent of the closure becomes evident. The entry from the road on the other side of the courtyard is completely sealed with breezeblock, darkening the whole aspect of the place – already depressing enough from the total lack of industry.

Within the distillery the same atmosphere prevails. Only one entry door

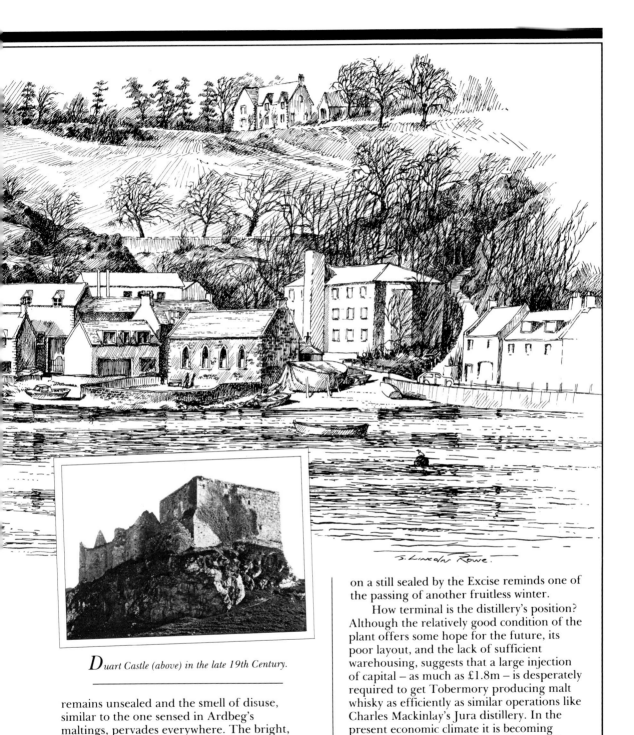

S. Lincoln Rowe.

*D*uart Castle (above) in the late 19th Century.

remains unsealed and the smell of disuse, similar to the one sensed in Ardbeg's maltings, pervades everywhere. The bright, airy stillhouse presents a more cheering picture, although a discreet autumn leaf lying on a still sealed by the Excise reminds one of the passing of another fruitless winter.

How terminal is the distillery's position? Although the relatively good condition of the plant offers some hope for the future, its poor layout, and the lack of sufficient warehousing, suggests that a large injection of capital – as much as £1.8m – is desperately required to get Tobermory producing malt whisky as efficiently as similar operations like Charles Mackinlay's Jura distillery. In the present economic climate it is becoming increasingly unlikely that Tobermory will ever produce malt whisky again.

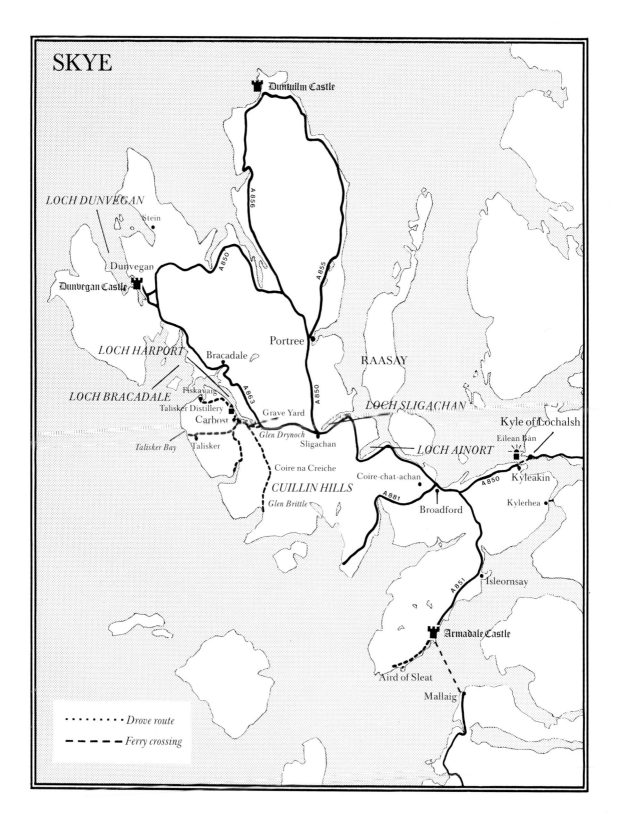

SKYE

Duntuilm Castle

LOCH DUNVEGAN

Stein

Dunvegan

Dunvegan Castle

LOCH HARPORT

Bracadale

LOCH BRACADALE

Fiskavaig

Talisker Distillery

Carbost

Talisker Bay   Talisker

Portree

RAASAY

Glen Drynoch   Sligachan

LOCH SLIGACHAN

Kyle of Lochalsh

Eilean Bàn

LOCH AINORT

Kyleakin

Coire na Creiche   Coire-chat-achan

CUILLIN HILLS

Glen Brittle

Kylerhea

Broadford

Isleornsay

Armadale Castle

Aird of Sleat

Mallaig

A 856

A 850

A 855

A 863

A 850

A 881

A 850

A 851

Grave Yard

·········· *Drove route*

− − − − *Ferry crossing*

CHAPTER SIX

SKYE

CONFLICTING SOCIAL FORCES left their mark on the Hebrides in the late 18th and early 19th Centuries. The production of kelp was one of the most important factors governing the prosperity of the population. During the height of the Napoleonic War the price of the precious commodity (used mainly in the production of glass) was driven to £20 a ton, but out of this sum the kelpers received precious little, with the greater part of the sale price being pocketed by the laird. The Jura historian John Mercer disapprovingly recorded: *T*HE KELPERS . . . WERE NOT AL-*lowed to work for themselves, but had to pass their produce to the owners, the latter usually paying them about 15 per cent of their own receipts; the kelp left in their chartered vessels, the buyers not being encouraged to visit the islands. The owners benefitted by the increasing over-population, for this meant more kelpers, with the latter's slowly rising incomes allowing parallel increases in their rents. The kelpers were told when and which beds to cut, according to their status in the tenant hierarchy.*

However, the tide of emigration to North America gradually rose after the kelp boom, when restrictions on the import of Spanish barilla (which yielded five times more alkali than kelp) were lifted after Napoleon's defeat. Prior to this, the parish of Bracadale in Skye had produced some 50 tons of kelp per year (20 tons of seaweed yielded 1 ton of kelp), and this modest amount tended to stem the tide of emigration while kelping remained a profitable enterprise for the laird. But, ultimately, there were too many mouths to feed after the War, particularly with 'the return of great numbers of persons formerly employed in the Navy and Army,' and many appeals were made to the Government by the Hebridean landowners whose profits from kelp were diminishing by the year.

The principal Liverpool kelp agents W A and G Maxwell summarised the state of the industry from 1817 to 1828 by calculating that from the sale of a ton of kelp in 1818 at £8 0s 0d the profit to the landlord was £4 7s 6d after deductions of £2 10s 0d for 'price of manufacture', 13s 0d for freight, and 9s 6d for the agent's charge. By 1828, a ton of kelp fetched only £3 13s 4d, yielding the landlord just 10d after similar deductions.

Inevitably, many tenants were unceremoniously cleared from the land to make way for the hardy cheviot sheep – in Skye these clearances were often carried out with little humanity. Many of the emigrants arrived in North America to find that there was little enough room for them, and only the fortunates were provided with ground.

Even as late as 1830 it was calculated that only by abolishing the tax on window glass could the kelp industry be relieved, but by then it was beyond help and the population in Bracadale gradually receded. By 1825 a couple of new faces appeared in the parish, Hugh and Kenneth MacAskill from Eigg. They implemented the new and unpopular system of farming which the Reverend Roderick MacLeod succinctly described as 'throwing a number of farms into one large tack for sheep-grazing, and dispossessing and setting adrift the small tenants.'

Having arrived in Skye, Hugh acquired the tack of Talisker House in 1825 where Johnson and Boswell had stayed with Colonel MacLeod of MacLeod during their visit to the region. The name was derived from the 'Echo Rock' or Talamh Sgeir on the shore of Loch Harport. He cleared the crofters from his lands, and replaced them with sheep – those who remained did so in poverty. The Reverend MacLeod wrote: *THE HABITS OF THE people are far from cleanly . . . there were 140 families found in the parish who had no change of night or day clothes . . . (however, the people) . . . are shrewd and sagacious, and manifest a good degree of intellect as to the ordinary affairs of life; as to morality and religion, it is yet but a day of small things . . . (The farming system had) . . . placed them in such absolute dependence on the tacksmen, as to preclude any hope of amelioration.*

The MacAskills were clearly of some means and expanded their interests in 1830 by obtaining a 1 acre feu at 30s per annum for 60 years, and a further 20-acre allotment on the shore of Loch Harport at Carbost. Kenneth was by now the bank agent in Portree and was probably instrumental in raising the capital – the considerable sum of £3,000 – which they used to build a distillery on the tack – naturally enough, named Talisker. Kenneth was listed as the licensee in 1833, acting as manager and producing malt whisky of good quality with a ready local market. The Rev MacLeod – a passionate, evangelical preacher – upheld temperance zealously and had no doubts as to the effects of dram drinking on his parishioners. In Bracadale were: *FIVE licensed whisky houses; and whisky is retailed in various other places within the parish, to the manifest injury of the temporal interests of the people, and the progressive and sure destruction of their morals.*

He went on to conclude his report in a manner which betrayed his bearing in the pulpit: *THE MOST STRIKING VARIATIONS betwixt the present state of the parish and that which existed at the time of the last Statistical Account, are 1. The formation of a Parliamentary road, which goes nearly over it's whole length: 2. The system of farming for some time followed, of several farms being thrown into one grazing; 3. The erection and establishment of a whisky distillery, The first of these variations is a decided benefit to the parish; the second, as decided a disadvantage to its general population; and the third, one of the greatest curses which, in the ordinary course of Providence, could befall it or any other place.*

Since the MacAskills were in the traditional mould of island farmer-distillers with varying interests, they were able to survive the poor harvests and bad weather which beset the late 1830s and early 1840s causing haphazard production and many distillery closures. Between 1836 and 1843, the consumption of spirits in Scotland dropped from 6.6 to 5.6 million gallons (30 to 25.4 million litres) – 90% of this was malt whisky.

Despite the reputation of its product, on the death of Kenneth in 1854, Talisker was put up for sale at the knockdown price of £1,000, reflecting the depressed state of the malt industry which had continued to suffer from the competition of the large Lowland pot still whisky producers.

Eventually, in 1863, the year of Hugh's death, the distillery lease was transferred to his son-in-law Donald MacLennan, but his

*The fertile shores of Loch Harport (above)
provided the MacAskill brothers with the
farming base from which they expanded their interests
to establish Talisker Distillery
(insert) in the early 1830s.*

business was sequestrated soon after and it was not until 1868 that the Talisker lease came into the hands of Anderson & Co. J R W Anderson's business lasted 8 years before being dissolved. He was not an entirely honest trader, being found guilty in 1880 of defrauding whisky merchants into believing he had placed whisky in bonded warehouses for them.

Roderick Kemp & Co, in partnership with Alexander Grigor Allan, took over the distillery for just over £1,800 and it was once more in respectable hands. Kemp, on the one hand, was in the wine and spirit trade in Aberdeen, while Allan was one of the owners of Glenlossie Distillery.

By 1880 the reputation of Talisker was such that Kemp and Allan immediately started a comprehensive programme of modernisation at a time when Jura distillery had just been rebuilt. On Islay, Lochindaal was similarly being remodelled while Bruichladdich and Bunnahabhain were just being established.

Around the same time the formation of The Distillers Company Ltd took place

amongst the six major Lowland grain distillers to rationalise competition and regulate prices – their control of the industry was ultimately to reach as far as Talisker.

Alfred Barnard was one of the first to observe the improvements, reporting that the plant contained 'all the newest appliances and vessels known in the art of distilling.' He also recorded that: *S*MALL

steamers, or as they are called 'puffers', come up the loch to within fifty yards of the granaries. These bring barley and stores used in the works; and besides this, the 'Hebridean' from Glasgow, a deep sea steamer calls once a week.

Barnard probably did not witness the loading of casks onto the puffers, and would therefore have been unable to realise the problems which the lack of a pier at the distillery caused. These came to a head in 1891 when Kemp unsuccessfully petitioned his laird, MacLeod of Dunvegan to allow a pier to be constructed, stating that it would be '. . . an immense facility for our business.' Ideally Kemp wanted a feu for the distillery so as not to compromise any further investment, such as a pier, that he might make in the distillery. He continued: *W*HEN A STEAMER CALLS, WHICH most frequently is in the middle of the night, we have to float out the whisky into the loch for a distance of 3 to 4 hundred yards, and towed by means of ropes and a small boat in order to get it on board. The difficulty and danger of doing this, especially in a dark and stormy night, no one can imagine except those who witness the operation.

I have no doubt you have heard of the celebrated Glenlivet Distillery which is on the Duke of Richmond and Gordon's land and which is entailed like your own. The Distillery has hitherto been tenanted by a lease, but lately His Grace granted the tenant a feu on no other consideration but a very moderate rent for the ground.

After consulting with his lawyer in Portree, MacLeod (who was often unavailable in Paris) declined to grant Kemp a feu or the right to build a pier even after Kemp offered to supply all the materials. His correspondence with MacLeod betrayed a growing desperation: *. . . A* NUMBER OF *people in attempting to board the steamer in the bay, narrowly escaped perishing. On this occasion we lost a valuable stock of whisky and between 30 and 40 empty casks which were sent to the Distillery for filling. Consider the magnitude of this loss alone to us.*

Finally he stated that the lack of a pier was '. . . paralysing and deteriorating our business to a most serious extent,' and losing patience with MacLeod he sold out to his partner A G Allan in 1892 when the business was valued at £25,000.

Kemp bought the Macallan Distillery and Allan took over the business as a leasehold (at £110 per annum) with a rent of £23 12s for the surrounding tack and a 10 gallon cask of malt for the laird! It was incorporated in December 1894 as The Talisker Distillery Ltd with stock in bond valued at £7,202 in June of that year. An issue of 2,000 preference shares of £10 each and 20,000 ordinary £1 shares was made which were bought up by a wide variety of interests, although Allan retained ultimate control until his death in 1895.

The lease was then transferred by his trustees to the Talisker Distillery Co Ltd which operated successfully until 1898 when a resolution to wind it up was passed. Officially this finally took place in 1900,

*O*ne of the Cuillins looms out of the cloud and mist providing an eerie backdrop to the famous three-arched bridge at Sligachan on the road to Carbost.

although by then the company had merged with the Dailuaine-Glenlivet Co to form Dailuaine-Talisker Distilleries Ltd. Under Thomas Mackenzie the distillery was extended in 1900, and a pier finally built and connected to the distillery by tramway. At the same time distillery houses were erected for workers and excise officers, reflecting the trend established at Bunnahabhain and Caol Ila.

Mackenzie was a capable distiller who had enlarged Dailuaine until it was the largest Highland malt distillery in operation. He was also one of the forces behind the establishment of Imperial distillery, and the associated warehousing at Carron in the late 1890s during the boom in malt production. Surprisingly, Imperial was closed in 1899 and did not re-open until 1919.

His death in March, 1915, when firms like Buchanan and Dewar were on the verge of amalgamating and the recession in the trade was leading to the merging of many smaller companies into the larger operators, led to the eventual takeover of Dailuaine-Talisker Distilleries Ltd after their board had approached William Ross of the DCL for advice.

In 1915 Ross had chaired meetings amongst the leading Highland malt distillers in an attempt to discuss the possibilities of rationalisation amongst them. Despite the failure of these negotiations, the whole of the shares of Dailuaine-Talisker Distilleries was purchased by the DCL, John Dewar and Sons Ltd, W P Lowrie and Co Ltd, and John Walker and Sons Ltd.

This takeover represented one of the first incursions by the DCL into the world of malt whisky production. It was not that they were acquiring a taste for this sector, merely that, under the guidance of William Ross, they were now administering a sharp medicine to the trade as a whole which he believed would effect a long lasting cure.

Talisker finally entered the DCL fold proper in 1925, effectively making Dailuaine-Talisker Distilleries Ltd a wholly-owned subsidiary. The distillery remained licensed to Dailuaine-Talisker until 1930 when operation was transferred to SMD. It was not to experience a change in licensee until 1982 when Dailuaine-Talisker Distilleries Ltd was voluntarily wound up and taken over by SMD, who transferred the licence to John Walker & Sons Ltd. Their familiar trademark was inconspicuously introduced to the Talisker malt label, leaving the product's familiar image relatively unchanged.

More fundamental change has altered the distillery itself since the SMD takeover. Having dropped triple distillation in 1928, the distillery remained unaltered until 1960 when fire destroyed the entire stillhouse forcing the first shutdown since World War II. Perfect replicas of the five stills were installed as the distillery was rebuilt. These externally coal-fired items were eventually to be converted to the more common internal steam-coil heating in 1972 when the malting floors were demolished as malted barley began arriving from the mainland.

Now, the entire distillery, bar the manager's house, warehouses and offices are post 1960. Despite its apparent youth, one traditional feature has remained intact – the condensers. The modern, compact and efficient condensers seen in the great majority of distilleries are absent at Talisker, instead the spirit passes down the lyne arms of the five stills to traditional worm tubs outside the stillhouse. Water carried along a lade from the Carbost burn keeps the tubs brim full of cooling water. It is an archaic feature perhaps, but it never breaks down and gives the visitor a better understanding of the way in which distilleries traditionally operated.

Talisker is now one of the few home market malts bottled at a higher than normal alcoholic strength at 45.8% volume instead of 40% and this has lent it an image of being something of a man's malt — robust and strong. Neil Gunn, however, pointed out its only drawback when he said, 'At its best it can be superb, but I have known it to adopt the uncertainties of the Skye weather.'

This is certainly true, but it must be said that at its best, it is quite simply the very best.

TALISKER DISTILLERY
CARBOST, ISLE OF SKYE

Owners:
SCOTTISH MALT DISTILLERS LTD

TRINITY RD, ELGIN
MORAYSHIRE IV30 1UF

Licensees:
JOHN WALKER & SONS LTD

63 ST JAMES' ST
LONDON SW1A 1NB

Manager:
DEREK BOTTOMER

Telephone: 047842 203

(Visits should be arranged through the
SMD at the Elgin office.
Telephone: 0343 7891)

The conventional road to Skye takes in the short crossing from Kyle of Lochalsh to Kyleakin (Haco's Strait), where the Norwegian fleet anchored in 1263, and passes into a region of Skye where Norse associations abound. Although the island is only a short distance from the mainland, it is like another world – the most uncompromising and atmospheric in the Hebrides.

Caisteal Maoil c. 1900 (above).
The Clan Donald Centre (far right).

The remains of Caisteal Maoil stand close to the shore where, it is believed, a Norse princess levied a toll on passing ships. She effected this by spanning the strait with a length of chain. This was tethered on the Skye side to a small stone pillar standing on the foreshore about a mile west of the castle and opposite the lighthouse, which is reputedly haunted. When the Norsemen eventually quit Skye (perhaps leaving a few of their spirits behind), the Mackinnons entered the castle under the patronage of the Lords of the Isles.

The other crossings to Skye are less convenient but offer more flexibility for the visitor, and will continue to do so until a

bridge, if ever, is built at Kyleakin. A passenger ferry operates during the summer months between Glenelg on the mainland and Kylerhea – this is the point at which Johnson and Boswell crossed, and used to be the focal point of the droving operations for the cattle leaving Skye for the London markets. The current is swift here and Hugh Miller described the passage of the yacht *Betsey* through the waters as '. . . like a cork caught during a thunder shower in one of the rapids of the High Street.'

Johnson and Boswell, however, had an uneventful crossing, and having dis-embarked, journeyed down to the ancestral home of the MacDonalds at Armadale, which is now the landing point for the other vehicle ferry crossing to Skye from Mallaig. This crossing offers greater scope for the traveller wishing to see a larger part of Skye, since the road to Carbost will mean that he must literally make his way around the Cuillins to Loch Harport.

The A851 retraces Johnson and Boswell's route north by Isle Ornsay and from there to Broadford where the A850

joins from Kyleakin, some 8 miles (13 km) distant. Before they crossed to Raasay, Johnson and Boswell stayed at Coire-chat-achan in the shadow of Beinn na Caillich (732 metres) and received the same splendid hospitality as one of the previous guests, Thomas Pennant. Here, Johnson witnessed the effects of over-indulgence in dram drinking when Boswell was unable to raise himself from his bed until noon the next day.

Johnson, for his part, had become more than a little familiar with one of the married ladies on the previous evening, but it was unlikely that whisky was responsible, for he only once tried it '. . . at the inn in Inveraray,

when I thought it preferable to the English malt brandy. It was strong, but not pungent, and was free from the empyreumatic taste or smell. What was the process I had no opportunity of inquiring, nor do I wish to improve the art of making poison pleasant.'

He gave a complete record of the Hebridean diet in such a household, and remarked that the man of the house '. . . as soon as he appears in the morning, swallows a glass of whisky; yet they are not a drunken race, at least I never was present at much intemperance; but no man is so abstemious as to refuse the morning dram, which they call a skalk.'

Talisker Bay, where Sam Johnson and James Boswell (above) arrived during their tour of the Hebrides in 1774 to stay at Talisker House, with Col MacLeod of MacLeod.

They consumed a large variety of drink whilst in Skye, including port, claret, punch brandy, Scotch porter and Holland's gin, but Johnson according to Boswell, never drank fermented liquor. From Coire-chat-achan, they made their way via Broadford to Raasay Island as guests of MacLeod of Raasay, where they were received with '. . . nothing but civility, elegance and plenty.'

Incidentally, in 1843, Anderson's 'Guide' noted that 'Broadford consists of only three houses and the hotel and the inn, which is a comfortable one. The charges, as in most parts of Skye are moderate. In one article only are they higher than in the mainland highlands, namely, whiskey, of which not a drop is made in Skye, either by smuggler or regular distiller.' The author obviously hadn't ventured as far as Carbost, where he would have found the decade-old distillery, and he had most certainly not bumped into the Reverend MacLeod.

Johnson and Boswell eventually made their way to Talisker by way of Portree and Dunvegan. The present-day road from Broadford continues along the eastern shore by way of Loch Ainort, before turning down Loch Sligachan where it forks at the head of the loch. The A850 continues to Portree, while the A863 leads through Glen Drynoch to Loch Harport, passing by the ancient burial ground of the MacLeods of Drynoch at the end of the loch. At the turn of the century the Reverend MacCulloch of Portree described it as being 'grisly and gaunt and cheerless, as if a curse rested on it.' The more cheerful prospect of Talisker distillery lies close to the shore, beyond Carbost village.

A new reception room for visitors now houses many Talisker artifacts, and is an interesting education for those newly introduced to the world of malt whisky. More recent alterations include the restoration of the office building to its original condition – it being one of the few buildings not destroyed in the fire of 1960.

Derek Bottomer, the manager, often guides visitors around, pointing out the original low-roofed warehouses, (in which, some locals claim, there are still unclaimed casks from before World War II), the odd number of stills, five in this case, and those curious worm tubs behind the stillhouse – simple but effective.

The original intended site of the MacAskill's distillery is to be found 5 miles (8 km) further north of the current location at Fiskavaig, just beyond Portnalong but an unreliable water source forced the brothers to settle for Carbost. A tour around the surrounding countryside is the perfect way to get the most out of a visit to a distillery like Talisker. Over the back of the village some 6 miles (9.6 km) distant, along a bleak moorland road which basks in the grandeur of the distant Cuillins, lies Talisker House where Colonel MacLeod received Johnson and Boswell.

Talisker is sheltered in one of the most suprising glens in Skye, a gentle bowl hemmed in by steep slopes leading down to the sea presenting a perfect view west to the Outer Hebrides. Johnson, however, saw nothing of the sort and remarked that, 'Talisker is the place, beyond all that I have seen, from which the gay and the jovial seem utterly excluded; and where the hermit might expect to grow old in meditation, without possibility of disturbance or interruption'.

Granted, on the worst of days the place might be forboding but it seems the perfect spot to end a tour of the Hebridean distilleries, a gentle haven amongst the bleak surrounding countryside, and one in which Johnson, by his own admission, never allowed himself to be enamoured of the local spirit – a rule which over 2 centuries later the present-day traveller is wise to ignore.

The sheltered setting of Talisker House.

BIBLIOGRAPHY

Andrews, Allen *The Whisky Barons*, Jupiter Books, 1977

Barnard, Alfred *The Whisky Distilleries of the United Kingdom*, Harper's weekly Gazette, 1887

Barnett, Ratcliffe *Autumns in Skye, Ross and Sutherland*, John Grant, 1946

Boswell, James *The Tour to the Hebrides*, second edition, London, 1785

Brander, Michael *A Guide to Scotch Whisky*, Johnston & Bacon, Edinburgh, 1975

Budge, Donald *Jura, An Island of Argyll*, Smith & Son, 1960

Cooper, Derek *Skye*, Routledge and Kegan Paul, 1970

Cooper, Derek and Godwin, Fay *The Whisky Roads of Scotland*, Jill Norman & Hobhouse, 1982

Crick, Bernard *George Orwell, A Life*, Secker & Warburg, 1980

Daiches, David *Scotch Whisky, Its Past and Present*, Andre Deutsch, 1969

Daiches, David *Scotland and The Union*, John Murray, 1977

Donaldson, Gordon *Scottish Historical Documents*, Scottish Academic Press, 1970

Geikie, Sir Archibald *Scottish Reminiscences*, Maclehose, 1904

Gordon, Anne Wolrige *Dame Flora*, Hodder & Stoughton, 1974

Haldane, A R B *The Drove Roads of Scotland*, Thos Nelson & Sons, 1952

House, Jack *The Spirit of White Horse*, Capricorn Arts, 1971

Hume, John R *The Industrial Archaeology of Scotland, The Highlands and Islands*, (Gen Ed: K Falconer), Batsford, 1977

Johnson, Samuel *A Journey to the Western Islands of Scotland*, 1774

Knox, John *A tour through the Highlands of Scotland and the Hebride Isles in 1784*, London, 1787

Laver, James *The House of Haig*, John Haig & Co, 1958

Lockhart, Sir Robert Bruce *Scotch, The Whisky of Scotland in Fact and Story*, Putnam, 1951

MacCulloch, J A *The Misty Isle of Skye*, Eneas Mackay, 1931

MacCulloch, John *The Highlands and Western Isles of Scotland*, London, 1824

MacCulloch, John *A description of the Western Islands of Scotland*, Constable, 1819

Macdonald, James *General View of the Agriculture of the Hebrides or Western Isles of Scotland*, 1811

MacGregor, Alasdair Alpin *The Western Isles*, Robert Hale, 1949

Martin, Martin *A Description of the Western Islands of Scotland*, Andrew Bell, London, 1703

Maxwell, Gavin *Raven Seek Thy Brother*, Longmans, Green, 1968

McPhee, John *The Crofter and the Laird*, Farrar Straus & Giroux, 1970

Mercer, John *Hebridean Islands, Colonsay, Gigha, Jura*, Lealt Press, 1982

Miller, Hugh *The Cruise of the Betsey*, William Nimmo, 1870

Mitchell, Joseph *Reminiscences of my life in the Highlands*, 1883, rprt, David & Charles, 1971

Morewood, Samuel *A Philosophical and Statistical History of the Inventions and Customs of Ancient and Modern Nations in the Manufacture and Use of Inebriating Liquors*, Dublin, 1838

Morrice, Philip *The Schweppes Guide to Scotch*, Alphabooks, 1983

Moss, M & Hume, John R *The Making of Scotch Whisky*, James & James, 1981

Pennant, Thomas *A Tour in Scotland and Voyage to the Hebrides 1772*, 1774

Pyke, Magnus *Science and Scotch Whisky*, The Distillers Company plc

Ramsay, Freda *John Ramsay of Kildalton*, Peter Martin, Toronto, 1970

The Scotch Whisky Association, *Scotch Whisky: Questions and Answers*

Sillett, S W *Illicit Scotch*, Beaver, 1965

Simpson, W Douglas *The Ancient Stones of Scotland*, Robert Hale, 1968

Sinclair, Sir John *The Statistical Account of Scotland drawn up from the communications of the ministers of the different parishes*, 1794, vol XX

Spiller, Brian *DCL Distillery Histories Series*, 1981

The Statistical Account of Scotland, 1845, vol VII, XVI

The Stent Book and Acts of the Balliary of Islay, 1718–1843, 1890

Storrie, Margaret C *Islay, Biography of an Island*, Oa Press, 1981

Wilson, John *Scotland's Malt Whiskies*, Famedram, 1973

Wilson, John *Scotland's Distilleries*, Famedram, 1980

Wilson, Ross *Scotch Made Easy*, Hutchinson, 1959

Wilson, Ross *Scotch, The Formative Years*, Constable, London, 1970

INDEX